HARVESTING THE EDGE

BIOGRAPHICAL NOTE

G.F.Dutton, born in 1924 of Anglo-Scottish parentage on the borders of Wales, has travelled the globe but spent most of his life among the passionate austerities, urban and rural, of Scotland. He has from the beginning felt compelled to explore our environment, inner and outer, and this has led to – among other things – a number of publications, mostly on medical science (for which he has received international honours), but also mountaineering (the two 'hilarious classics', *The Ridiculous Mountains*, reprinted Hodder 1990, *Nothing so Simple as Climbing*, Hodder 1993), wild-water swimming (*Swimming Free*, Heinemann and St.Martin's Press 1972) and verse. The verse, published in various reviews and anthologies, includes the prize-winning collections *Camp One* (Macdonald 1978), *Squaring the Waves* (Bloodaxe Books 1986) and *The Concrete Garden* (Bloodaxe Books 1991), a Poetry Book Society Recommendation. For thirty five years he has been based in a rather exiguous house among boulders and blasts of wind in the south-eastern Highlands where he has built up a remarkable wild 'marginal' garden – known to many through his series of articles in the Journal of the Royal Horticultural Society (*The Garden*); it has also been featured in BBC television's 'Gardener's World'. The reason for these various explorations – and their essential unity – is itself explored in the present book. He admits to many other interests, including a family.

HARVESTING THE EDGE

Some Personal Explorations from a Marginal Garden

G. F. Dutton

Menard Press

1995

Harvesting the Edge

1994 © G. F. Dutton

Cover design by Merlin James
Design, setting and camera ready copy by Lijna Minnet

Representation and distribution in UK:
Central Books (Troika),
99 Wallis Road,
Hackney Wick,
London E9 5LN
Tel: 0181-986 4854

Distribution in rest of the world apart from North America:
Central Books

Distribution in North America:
SPD Inc
1814 San Pablo Avenue
Berkeley, CA 94702, USA

ISBN: 1 874320 01 2

The Menard Press
8 The Oaks
Woodside Avenue
London N12 8AR
Tel: 0181-446 5571

Printed at Alden Press
Oxford and Northampton

ACKNOWLEDGEMENTS

Grateful acknowledgements are made to Neil Astley of Bloodaxe Books and to Callum Macdonald, the publisher of *Camp One*, for formal permission to quote the author's verse published in book form; to the editors of *Active in Airtime, The Garden* (Journal of the Royal Horticultural Society), *Lines Review* and *Malahat Review* for other published verse or prose of the author; to Messrs Faber and Faber, and Routledge and Kegan Paul, for quotations from work by Wallace Stevens, W. C. Williams and K. H. Jackson respectively; to Robin Fulton for many things including his translation of Olav Hauge; and among others, especially to Leslie Bisset, James Hogan, John Kernohan, Anne Stevenson and Alan Wall for ideas literary, horticultural or simply helpful; to Anthony Rudolf for suggesting this book be written and for enthusiasm throughout; to my family for helping to maintain garden and gardener at periods of climatic crisis; and to the memory of M. W.-M. who at the very beginning believed in our belief and provided the grounds for it.

PUBLISHER'S PREFACE

It is unusual for a publisher to write a preface to a book but in this case there was a good reason. G.F.Dutton has published many articles in the Journal of the Royal Horticultural Society about his extraordinary marginal garden and has, indeed, completed a book based on them – as yet unpublished. Those writings are aimed at a horticulturally sophisticated audience. It is to prevent confusion that I wish to explain the circumstances of this book, one of four published on the occasion of Menard's 25th birthday.

For many years my friend and associate James Hogan has told me stories about G.F.Dutton (the initials are not a Leavisite affectation but serve to distinguish our author from his namesake the Australian poet Geoffrey Dutton), which intrigued me and built up my curiosity. Furthermore, he showed me G.F.D.'s poems and suggested there was a certain affinity between them and my own, which there was. So, when I told James I would be spending a month in Scotland at the end of 1993 he set up the meeting. I duly drove north from Hawthornden Castle to take a look at this "poet's garden", this "garden's poet".

I shall not rhapsodise about my day with Geoffrey, except to say that it was one of the most moving and fascinating experiences of my life. So much so that when I got back to the Castle (after an unpleasant drive including a stretch of zero-visibility fog), I phoned him and suggested he write a book about his garden for my constituency, that is to say people who are more likely to have read G.F.D.'s Bloodaxe poetry books or selections in anthologies than his learned articles in the JRHS.

G.F.D. was very pleased to be asked but said he needed time to think about it. I hoped against hope he would agree. The two-way feedback between his garden and his poetry, the emotional and intellectual power emanating from this threefold creator (a scientist of international renown as well as being a gardener and poet of distinction) as he walked/talked me through his nine-acre multiple eco-system on a snowy December day, screamed into my old publisher's brain: book, book, book. He agreed. Here it is.

I am inordinately pleased that he was persuaded to tell us his story. It records the knowledge of a lifetime, knowledge we can call wisdom when we come to realise that, for him, the landscape incorporates its interpreter. At the same time we realise that in the scrupulous and loving accuracy of his observations, the poet and scientist are one. He has earned the right to "argue that making this garden is writing a poem, and walking the paths, reading it. And like a poem, only partly composed by oneself: the structure is there, waiting to offer its message, to be framed as 'epiphanies', compartments of happening, to communicate with the planter – who will fit his plants to it like words chosen for the correct place, and delete the weeds". G.F.D. writes in his verse about the interface between human and wild nature, and demonstrates in his garden their inseparable partnership. This book brings it all together, a poem in prose which will outlive him and us, and outlive his garden: "you must pay for the privilege of life, and gardening is the most transient of arts".

Anthony Rudolf, 1994

AUTHOR'S PREFACE

This is not a proper gardening book. Gardening concerns both head and hands. This little book – really an essay – concerns only the head, and the top of the head at that.

Partly it has been quarried from a proper gardening book – all of the head and both dirty hands – as yet unpublished, partly also from cleaner-fingered passages of published horticultural articles – themselves extracted from that ample and uncomplaining Epic.

Quite often, it treats gardening as just one of several explorations I have pursued or been led along; and the interest of that to gardeners depends on the height of their hedges and the degree of their forbearance.

For non-gardeners – to whom it is principally addressed – I have tried to ensure that the only Latin name of any plant occurs in a poem or the title of one.

For myself, writing it has been another informative exploration, begun by kind request and conducted I can only hope at no one else's undue expense.

G. F. Dutton, 1994

CONTENTS

no symbols where none intended
Samuel Beckett

COMMON GROUND

Like any animal, when released from the nest, or the cage, I began to explore. Cautiously; a sniff here; and there; a retreat; an advance. I collected sense data from the external environment and, when they gave the internal me pleasure, I sniffed again and pursued that particular path to collect more.

So I claim no originality over the rat. But for the better introduction of this book let me briefly record three or four explorations relevant to it: first, of the outer environment, then of the inner. They usefully extend our more routine daily patrols.

I found especial pleasure in exploring mountain country at all seasons – call it mountaineering; or the surface and shallow depths of seas, rivers or lakes with mask, fins and snorkel – call it wild-water swimming. In various parts of the world. These trips (the word has acquired a convenient further meaning) delivered fairly vigorous bundles of sensory data, and I enjoyed the challenge of disciplining my response to them so that I stayed sufficiently alive to bring in more.

Born not only an animal but a human being in addition, I explored at the same time the internal environment, my genome as they say, examining the interplay there between these external data and my processing of them: whereby each additional impression changes irremediably, and is changed by, those preceding it. I suppose you can call such inner explorations science, or art, depending on whether the processing is imposed, or evoked.

It being easier to follow scientific explorations – which require a long apprenticeship and purse – at professional level, I became an experimental research scientist, striking a path which could broadly be termed molecular biology. There, every turn

1

brought exciting new data, possibilities to be collected, examined, tested underfoot as weight-bearing hypotheses, gingerly – and with many a rejection – stepped upon, to settle as stone after stone through the surrounding as yet Ineluctable; a progress mutually assisted by colleagues either side and across the globe – that did, yes, help to relieve suffering among others, and to ourselves brought minimal groceries but always a beckoning horizon. I found this kind of discovery and evaluation quite analogous to a roped climb up difficult rock and ice, or a solitary swim along an unknown coast: all of them intellectually demanding and imaginatively rich.

Similarly, I saw no conflict between these pursuits and that largely involuntary, less attributable, questing we term the arts. Several 'arts' are apparent in this book; including the practice of verse. Why verse?

Verse can be a very searching exploration. I read and write it as such. Any verse that bears weight on repeated re-reading is another stepping stone across the unknown. For verse is a peculiarly effective medium for poetry. Let me briefly, and rashly, enlarge on this.

I personally see verse as built to communicate: primarily with its constructor, or assembler, or even receiver (the further you hunt for its genesis, the further it flees) and secondarily through him with others, his listeners or readers.

Its structure is sufficiently tuneable, from rhythm, sound and typography, and from precision and economy of phrase, to communicate with an alerted recipient at higher efficiency than prose.

When tuned further, to the intensity of poetry, it should fashion from the whole explored environment – inner and outer – through insights that supplement or supplant prose logic, an artefact provocative enough to grasp the hand that holds it... (Miss Dickinson noted the removal of the top of her head under such circumstances, Housman prickles while shaving: there are countless other definitively personal tests – take your pick,

2

and prefer your own).

To vivisect poetry is unnecessary here and anyway best conducted under the partial anaesthetic of its own medium. Enough that I will occasionally quote stanzas of verse in these pages, employing them as illustrations: being more economical to print than the graphic kind, equally standing out from the text and, one hopes, as evocative to the reader. That most of them are my own is due to the publisher's specific request; and may be partially excused by their derivation from, and so marked relevance to, the personal activities being considered. They record my own incoming data, processed and selected to suggest how these various pursuits contribute to one creative experience. As maybe finding yourself the successful climber of a refractory peak, or the unexpected author of something you have long wanted to write.

above the plains
mountains flourish,
white, distracting eyes
at intersections.

they are cold, frequently
dangerous, always
exhausting and when you come down
are still there.

then why climb them?
ask your constituents
ask the headbellies ask
the paunchbrains, not knowing

what it is to represent them
what it is to be the guest
dirty, unapologetic
of even a minor pinnacle. [1]

Of only a single poem. And how this creative experience represents a permanent achievement, even if the flux flows around you apparently unchanged.

waves beat in,
rocks withstand;
this white ocean
this grey land

play creation
in the round
of the sun's leisure.
and I swim here

take my pleasure
not in sea
not in shore
but one clean stroke

after another.
that wave and rock
pick up, throw back
between them for ever. [2]

Perhaps I find harmony between these reasonably varied activities because, for better or worse, I grew up among metaphors,
always aware of a press of *Correspondances*, of Fenollosa's 'ho-
mologies, sympathies and identities.' Verse ties them together
on the page, and the kind of gardening I shall describe roots them
in common ground.

Recognising all this, and that every creative pursuit contrib-
utes to what Pound called the Nutriment of Society, I find self-
defeating the barricades built, and aggressively defended,
between Two Cultures, or Three, or between any of the parish
committees of art or science. Chemists, for example, may re-
mark sorrowfully of a colleague, 'He'll never understand that,
he's a Carbohydrate Man...'; and the West Point, or Orange
Lodge, initiation rites of some branches of medicine are as child-
ishly exclusive as those of certain schools of Art or Architec-

4

ture. These imaginary frontiers presumably reward what sloth or tyranny they shelter. The explorer travels freely from one discipline to the other, employing appropriate criteria for each; as leaving the Cuillin Ridge to swim through the kelp forests of Loch Scavaig[3] requires a certain change in equipment and technique. Excellence, or at least the competence to appreciate – or even allow for – excellence, is open to all who take the trouble.

So I suppose I reached inevitably a kind of synthesis. A productive coexistence of data from various lines of endeavour, all acting and reacting within. Somewhat claustrophobic? Not at all; and one can always liberate these players into an appropriate external theatre and sit back and watch. Appropriate, in being diverse enough to accommodate most of them, and to test them accordingly with stress and storm, whips and scorpions, or even Marianne Moore's toad, that impassive successor to the serpent in her imaginary garden.

Garden. We are there at last. A garden is an example of a suitable arena. For gardening is itself a synthesis of explorations, requiring the gardener to be craftsman, scientist and artist. Craftsman for physical dexterity and stamina, maintaining the garden; scientist for intellect, selecting its viable plants and keeping them healthy; and artist for imagination, ensuring it provides visual satisfaction. Also intelligent enough to keep these roles and qualities in balance: for a weak imagination can be overpowered by unremitting craftsmanship to give a trivial pretty-pretty display; or by a too forceful intellect (Yeats' 'will'), to offer mere rhetoric – blatant vistas and blinding colours.

One needs the balance. For gardens are supposed to bring Peace, as any horticultural calendar will testify. The peace is usually thought of as the peace of inaction. It never is, of course, and the actual peace, the only one compatible with *life*, is the peace maybe best found in a garden like the one I shall describe, the peace of equilibrium, a delicate – but not uneasy – balance of many kinds of force; from the awareness of which, and of the buffets it – and its gardener – receive, and absorb, I believe

5

one may approach a truer, possibly the true, peace; which Goethe recognises as 'a revelation emerging just where the inner world of man meets external reality.'

What, then of my particular garden? I term it, as you will discover, a Marginal Garden. Gardening by no means need entail digging and double-trenching like Thoreau on his bean–plot in Concord woods, who grossly fenced himself off and hedged himself in by that act; it can include mere felling of trees to make a vista across Walden Pond, as Emerson perpetrated on the same wood-lot: 'lot' – he had picked out, bought that land, and

> *Just to choose*
> *a corner of the wilderness*
> *is to enclose*
>
> *it with intent.*
> *Is to create*
> *garden, gardener*
>
> *a life spent*
> *cropping the rubble, a desire*
> *to regulate*
>
> *what goes by,*
> *catch at a scent, ensure*
> *some branch against the sky.*
>
> *Is to incur*
> *from the first day*
> *what creation cost, the haste*
>
> *to cut and tear,*
> *rake things over.*
> *At the least the need*
>
> *to look about, decide*
> *what wild flower*
> *is now a weed.* [4]

No small responsibility, a garden, however marginal.

UNTENABLE SKIES

No small responsibility either, to write about one. Fate – ever since Eden – tends to come down hard. Gardening literature is strewn with the consequences. Author after author through the centuries records, in rueful footnote or later edition, the rashly-provoked Cosmic Retort that pruned his pleasure. Many therefore cross themselves as they write, adding 'so far' or 'up to the present'. But I don't need to touch wood any more; I have grown enough of it around me. The place is now, after thirty-six or so years, rooted right through Time. If it, or I, or both, are obliterated tomorrow, it has *been*. In face of that, the entire spectrum of retribution, frost to fire, virus to vandal, is powerless. No more can waves wash away the fact that I swam through them.

I named this garden a Marginal Garden. Now we are outside the door we can examine tangible reasons for such a term.

To begin with, the land itself is classifiable as marginal, being at the limit of cultivation – a heap of boulders and dry glacial till above broken bedrock, reaching 900 feet altitude and open originally north and northwest to the most Arctic mountains in these islands. Their snowcaps keep a white eye on us for up to eight months of the year. We are balanced between glaciations. The climate is therefore appropriate, offering early and late frosts, short cool summers, long droughts, and severe winter cold. Further, this land is so dramatically featured and carries so attractive a natural vegetation that intensive gardening would ruin it. And finally because such horticultural excesses are fortunately prevented by the gardener himself being marginal. For I manage the place alone – and for twenty-five years did so only at weekends and occasional evenings, when not abroad. Now I have more time to dig and hack I grow less physically able; I remain a kind of curator, unable to interfere too disastrously.

Is so marginal a garden a garden at all? Why, yes. If a garden is worked or walked in for instruction and enjoyment, this one is as satisfying as any well-temperatured Elysium in Kerry, Cornwall, the wet Western Highlands, Lake Maggiore or wherever. For the natural forces operating here are so violent, the plants exploiting them so precisely selected, and the biological equilibrium therefore so finely poised, that a gardener is rapidly taught humility. Time and again upsetting it, he must escape to shelter, his presumptions blasted apart; and digest the lesson. He must always dig deeper than his spade. And the final picture he brings into being is, to himself at any rate, that much the more pleasurable.

Maybe at the raw beginning, as in many another novitiate, not faith but the challenge to it, holds him there.

> *they keep their distance*
> *although I planted them.*
> *although I protect them*
> *from slug, vole, the particular malice*
> *of climbing mice,*
> *the slash of pheasant.*
> *not to mention deer*
> *beyond the wire,*
> *in rut for the rust.*
>
> *flowers, flowers,*
> *from Oregon, from the Himalayas,*
> *bored with my bad soil*
> *reward my toil*
> *sparsely, are lost*
> *in deprecating leaves.*
> *my summer is what it achieves.*
> *were it not for the frost,*
> *rocks, teeth, rasping tongue,*
> *the living virulence I live among*
> *I would throw down*
> *spade and pen,*

cry off this slapped rump of a mountain.
go back to earnest discussion.
take a room in town. [1]

I described the site as dramatic. It is also remarkably varied. Within its three hectares – more or less, for it is so crinkled about that half a hectare could be lost in the folds – it carried turf and juniper, shadowy dens, heather moor and, splitting the place in two, a deep rocky thundering gorge with caves and waterfalls.

Given all that, why bother to garden at all? Well, it was not one of those places 'better', as that great gardener Gertrude Jekyll severely advised, 'left alone'. Most of the trees were broken and any regeneration grazed off. In ecological jargon, it was moribund.

A poor excuse. Why not leave it as such? Let it slide into boreal desert. And then stroll it, wolfing down, as on some favourite mountain, Emily Dickinson's 'banquet of abstemiousness'; or at least observe it uncovetously like Hudson or Jefferies or Daniel Boone, letting it flow through you.

The answer lies in another question – why did my hands itch? I had bought the ground for a house; already fenced it with Intent, beside which Rottweilers and live wire become afterthoughts. And even walking it, would tread out paths. Also, I had to bring up a family – for whom arctic storms needed tempering. The exploring animal must sometime dig its burrow.

So, the deed was done, the itching interfering hand would become a healing one, respecting the Genius of the Place. Three virile hours with a power saw could not be repaired within fifty years. Yet even careful restoration involves 'meddling' (another formidable Jekyllian rebuke), for winter shelter was essential to reinforce the tottering scrub and, as no shade-tolerant cold-resistant wind-proof tall evergreens grew naturally on the site (or in the British Isles), they had to be imported. Exploration, with possibly a vengeance; Avernus; Chernobyl; Sitka spruce.

I have implied that a site like this imposes firm discipline. The climate and what passes for soil strictly limit your choice of imports to those naturally selected by similar conditions abroad; but, happily, function determines form in plants as in poems, and such environmental next-of-kin usually look well with our natives.

The environment, in fact, determines the design of a marginal garden. This being a marginal wild hill garden, most of its vegetational framework must be of locals like birch and hazel, or exotics that will blend with them; so the picture will not clash with the splendidly muscular stride of landscape, which it therefore includes to mutual advantage. Any attempt to create a 'gardenesque' effect, such as Loudon described, where the imports – and the whole garden – differ as much as possible from the surroundings (say, no birch or hazel, but Indian chestnut, tulip tree and suchlike) is usually impossible here for physiological as well as aesthetic reasons – both these ends of our biological spectrum agreeing on that. A few of the tougher discordances might squeeze through climatically, like the more self-centred double blossoms or persistently exhibitionist foliage, but a Genius-consulting gardener debars as many purple passages as he can.

He also forbids too many kinds of plants in any one limited area, where their various leaves would squabble for room; or tall heavily-branched trees that might coarsen the scale of our canopies of birch and rowan.

For we can suffer frost any night of the year, being reasonably safe only from the third week in June to the third in August; so flowers are not our principal delight, but rather the shape and colour and shimmer of the leaves of trees and bushes. And since seven months of our deciduous year are leafless, also their bare boles and branch-tracery, against rock and rich conifers.

In matters of design like these, gardener and site work hand in hand; but the site dictates the garden's basic structure, and what must be planted where. You cannot impose yourself on such ground, so far north; in a wild garden, as in wild water, you swim with the current, never fight it, edging aside in your own direction whenever it lets you – Nature, that skilful swimmer Bacon observes, is commanded by obeying her. Pleasure comes not from free wishful-thinking, but from using the few resources given you in the most effective way; and finding that way in the first place.

I shall describe the site I was presented with.

The ground rises steeply a couple of hundred feet, due east. Above it, sheep and grouse moors, now edged obtrusively by forestry plantations, roll to a bare plateau of higher hills. Up the ground run two rocky defiles, one a former watercourse – call it the Dell – and the other a deep, sheer, virtually uncrossable ravine north of it – the Gorge – down which tumbles a small bouldery mountain river. So there are, north to south, five parcels of land stretching upwards: that north of the Gorge; the Gorge itself; between the Gorge and the Dell; the Dell itself; and south of the Dell.

Each is distinct from the others in soil and exposure, and therefore in vegetation, native or introduced. You can ascend any one of them along its own axis, absorbing its scenic and ecological character: respectively, highly-acid pine wood and heather moor; slightly basic moss-hung spray-forest; thin, acid, ericaceous birch woodland; lush neutral valley; and mildly acid juniper-dotted turf. Because of the knolly nature of the ground and its deliberate planting for shelter, each axis bears a chain of progressively revealed compartments, individually differing yet characteristic of that axis.

Certain great gardens, such as Hidcote or Sissinghurst[5], are arranged as a series of outdoor rooms, distinctively furnished between tall hedges. This marginal garden, much inferior in extent, climate and management, falls from its very nature into such a plan. Its compartments form suites of rooms, floored with moss, grass or heather and framed by rocks or the sheltering branchwork of trees and bushes. The design seeks to strengthen these episodes of surprise, or add to them; and always gently to modulate their interest along any particular axis.

However, you can switch axes by cross paths. And that brings the shock of immediate contrast – a plunge from heather moor to dripping caverns, from wild roses in the sun to mysterious bamboos and sultry rhododendrons. Diagonal cross-paths provide semi-tones of change.

So you can call on a virtually unlimited choice of horticultural, ecological or psychological experiences within a small area, simply by taking advantage of the site as it stands.

Of course I have indulged in more brazen, drawing-board, aesthetics, again encouraged by prevailing topographic drama. The three inner axes converge unexpectedly at a sudden emptiness; revealing a prospect – an *Ah, ah* – at which any 18th century devotee of the Sublime would have approvingly fluttered a cane.

You stand on a cliff-top in sun and wind. Immediately in front, the Gorge – here 150 feet across – drops with sheer or overhanging hundred-foot walls. The bare rock-faces opposite, equally high, carry flat heather moor. Invisible beneath, the river rumbles through thick jungle, but just upstream the Gorge is closed by a 60-foot barrier, down a cleft in which a waterfall thunders, of thirty-foot clear leap after rain. The cliffs echo with its landing, and ferns far below dodge and weave in the spray. Upstream, the Gorge winds tree-clad into distance, water creaming its rocks between diminishing cliffs.

This outlook is an unusual chance in a garden, worth exploiting as the culmination of the inner axes.

I must admit to another Visual Climax further up the Gorge, where the two outer axes, one of them the heather moor, meet... A stepped cascade, framed by leaning rowan trees, empties into a large dark cliff-surrounded pool; as evocative in autumn as the description of that one in the old Irish poem, where Froech swam back to Ailill, bearing red berries against white throat, black hair and white cheek.[6] One can sit and watch the circling water for hours.

The 18th century *cognoscenti* would find other familiar incidents in the garden. There is a Cave in the Gorge, though no hermit as yet; otters visit, and probably refugees from recurrent historical crises – Mons Graupius, Forteviot, Culloden;[7] it has a trout pool, for hurried breakfast, beside it. Ruins, too, of abandoned crofts; the grassy rooms of one have become garden compartments, humanised again. Many others, largely obliterated, lie about us.

> *not a random*
> *heap of stone –*
> *not on this green*
>
> *undulating meadow*
> *levelled*
> *just where it is.*
>
> *it has been*
> *carefully once*
> *walls and a roof, that gap*
>
> *marks the entrance*
> *and that rowan tree*
> *protected it from witches.*
>
> *three posts today*
> *keep the cattle*
> *from its dangerous well.* [2]

Let me repeat that whatever success this garden 'plan' has achieved in bringing pleasure to its few visitors, and intermittent satisfaction to myself, has not originated in my own efforts. I have – by taking away or adding vegetation – scooped out glades, accentuated valleys, heightened ridges, deepened hollows, flattened foregrounds; but the major effects have been dictated solely by the bones of topography and the need for shelter.

In one sense, then, this is a formal garden, where the stark framework of rock is treated as masonry, and planting employed to vivify, not confuse, it; the proportion of adornment to structure is crucial, needing a piety of restraint like that of the carved foliage on the columns of Southwell Chapter House; and I have kept well back, merely tried to help.

To help me help, the site ensures also ease of maintenance. I manage this area single-handed because the microenvironment of each axis largely gardens itself. Its indigenous plants thrive there through self-selection, and its exotics do so because they were chosen to suit it. 'Weeds' are minimal; in poor turfy places the locals stay neat on their spartan diet, and in (comparatively) richer spots groundcover, natural or introduced, keeps out undesirables, flowing between islands of more sybaritic specimens. Bare earth is impossible to maintain, appears artificial, encourages drought and lets in frost: the usual agreement between form, function and pleasure.

Of course there are periods of hard labour. This not being a horticultural treatise, I omit practical techniques worked out for such a moraine-encumbered site, delights though they must be to a Puritan.

> *You need a pointed spade*
> *for ground like this.*
>
> *To be of use*
> *in this last rock and turf.*
>
> *A square-edged blade*
> *so good to double-trench*
>
> *that first allotment*
> *would be bent*
>
> *never penetrate*
> *this kind of earth.*
>
> *You need to wrench*
> *then drive it straight*

lever to and fro
spoon up the stones

deep as you can go.
An inch or two to start

then once you're in,
no doubt.

But time, and finding soil to fill
the hole you've lifted out. [4]

And the sense of awe that guided our early, primitive, efforts
is not easily recaptured after living here so long.

stone.
like this one.
dug out years ago
when we were building the house.

we couldn't lift it
lever it, blast it so
it lies where we left it,
getting older

grey and silent,
gathering cracks;
eyes, eggs
seething beneath it

moss and ivy
eager beside it, already
lichen has tried it, it is marked
for life.

I remember it yellow, unblemished,
a growing refusal in the sunlight.
and us kneeling before it
sweating, dismantling its earth. [2]

We still need to move boulders, for planting. You can tell

from the sound of a boulder when struck how firmly and deeply it is embedded. If too large to lever out, a sledgehammer may disintegrate it; again, you learn from the sound if, and where, you may profitably strike. One only becomes aware of accumulated skill in these matters by observing the blood, sweat and tears of some unproductive Hercules. The boulders often lie in pure orange sand, final station of their fluvioglacial trek.

The whole site was moulded by Ice Ages, and the last readvance and its melt-back accost you, grossly or intimately, at every turn. The Dell, scoured by meltwater, still echoes vanished floods that smoothed rocks and scooped potholes; the Gorge was probably tunnelled along its fault by some subglacial torrent; and gravel-spreads, outwash fans, fluvial terraces and kames, ice-polished rock, ice-scratched rock, abound. One can walk the past along those ebb-tide shores of the great glacier-dammed lake that filled this glen and covered the lower slopes of the garden. It seems so recent. To and fro, to and fro, these monsters travelled, retreating sullenly some nine thousand years ago, leaving a moist sun-steamed nakedness for life to begin to begin upon, again.

> *Once more that sand is extended*
> *the glacier done, ended,*
> *the blue snout, the great ox-weight*
>
> *melted to silver and sunlight. Once more*
> *absence relaxes*
> *silence makes space.*
>
> *Before the return of the fuss.*
> *Before moss, grass*
> *and the marching rootmat*
>
> *before the rush*
> *of the first forests, before*
> *the first axes.* [4]

I described the dynamic equilibrium of plant, soil, and climate, and how dynamics – movement – govern the design: a progress up, down or between axis and axis. Progress not of course just in three dimensions (though this is decidedly a three-dimensional garden, on sunny days picked out in receding glitters of crag, ridge and hollow and on dull ones extinguished more abysmally than any flat ground): progress is four-dimensional.

Movement being so important here, a path is the first thing made. It holds the foreground together and assembles the distance. Around it, prospects must crystallise, successively. The observer travels along a path in Time, while the other three dimensions of the garden arrange themselves optimally about him.

You could never plan this place, let alone its paths, on paper. For instance, evergreens along a certain ridge contribute to design as well as shelter, continually contrasting with deciduous slopes behind. That interplay of busy coniferous needles and easy-going leaf trees might be guessed from a drawn plan, but not the subtleties revealed as you walk the nearby path: one texture sinks and the other rises, depending on the contours of the viewpoint. This kind of scheme, two-dimensional in pencil, three-dimensional on the ground, and four-dimensional while you walk, tends to satisfy at all seasons, and can only be worked out on the site itself.

Each path aims for the line of least resistance to eye and foot. It is dictated by the shape of the ground and by unyielding incidents like the trunk of a necessary tree or the fist of some great lichen-clad boulder. The path must be seen to take the only practicable pedestrian route up or down, in summer or in snow. If several possible routes exist, all but that selected are made less practicable: by extending a slope, introducing a rock or planting some resolute shrub. The paths are not paved or gravelled, but appear trodden ways, narrow or broad, melting into vegetation either side and recognised at once by their lack of obstruction, their moss, or their closer-mown turf. They are still,

and must unfortunately remain, sometimes interrupted by im-
moveable three-quarters buried boulders; but unlike their 18th
century Shenstonian counterparts, not by more overt moral in-
junctions.[8]

They are as natural to this garden as geometric walks are to a
frankly formal one; and should not be confused with the am-
biguous serpentine – the tempter – that tries to deny its own
stark limitations.

A kind of path
that won't pursue the truth
about a garden,

cannot square
with such severe
enclosure; but would rather

seek to please, gather
flowers, trees
repeat the views

of every daily
dilly-dallier. It lies
so easy, is so busy

setting out
sequence of avoidance
through the green plot that

a shock to find
suddenly its end
bare wire. And

maybe an iron gate.
To go further,
you open that. [4]

Which brings up a fairly basic duality of forces in a garden, less easily reconcilable than those already considered, and whose conflict, when controlled, helps to tune the Tension necessary for even a marginal attempt in art.

You have (especially in a place like this) constantly to balance the opposing demands of Imagination and Reason, Dionysius and Apollo, what you would like to do and what the site permits – the brain's task of censorship, resisting on a dive that longing to stay underwater, or analysing, at the laboratory bench of the Morning After, last night's over-inspired enthusiasms. In the garden, your compromise must be imaginatively reasonable – Concealing the Bounds by transfiguration, not deceit; employing technology to aid your pursuit, not divert it; choosing always the finer opulence of simplicity. If the dichotomy is extended to include the perennial Barbarian and Roman within us – whose eponyms skirmished often enough nearby – I try to be a minimally innovative barbarian, slave of neither extreme.

> *To carry long spears*
> *through a country of grass,*
>
> *wind washing over*
> *gold and silver,*
>
> *is no new thing*
> *has often been done*
>
> *will not shock the bog-cotton.*
> *This is an empire*
>
> *of grasses and air, far*
> *from the engines of Caesar, it will endure*
>
> *itch of the hand*
> *another time round. And as for us,*
>
> *though not of a mind*
> *for deep ores, precise furnaces,*

no loss; we understand
the white joy of platinum.

And follow the wind
with iron of our own. [4]

Another source of latent tension, spicing any equilibrium I bring about, is Time. You may regard each particular view from a path as a painting before you; so Gertrude Jekyll argued, and demonstrated. Moving a plant a few feet may, especially on this evocative ground, greatly increase its aesthetic 'significance' – like repositioning a word in a poem; the art connoisseur Leo Stein (brother of the other Gertrude) first appreciated Composition through discovering that a poppy in an actual meadow stood out simply because it grew beside a certain rock. But a poppy is an annual; it would be gone next year. Its colour on canvas would remain, and its name on the page. You must pay for the privilege of life, and gardening is the most transient of arts. Not only from the death of plants, but from their growth. Lawns can be mown, but trees rise tall, overpower horizontals and have to be felled or hideously lopped; or gathered with more pliable neighbours into a quite different composition. And of course we have gales: so must always be planting future stand-ins to take over smoothly.

The continuous creation of a succession of slowly-changing but always satisfying pictures is a fascinatingly difficult task; with many analogies. You live in, and for, the passing minute and yet plan seasons, infinite minutes, ahead. The skills of chess. Although the structure here may be fairly permanent, its gardener fashions upon it no more – and no less – than his own track through the waves.

And if, as here again, a garden's location is practically unvisited and its existence almost certain to cease with that of the gardener, it becomes a test case for the Purely Personal, of the

20

Selfish, in artistic justification. Then you may have difficulty in limiting Narcissism to the culture of daffodils.

Hence possibly my half-hearted attempts – like this one – to preserve part of it for others, even in a waterless vase.

Looking beyond aesthetics, this garden is an exploration I wished to undertake: living with a piece of country until I grew into it thoroughly, knowing it from bedrock upwards, ice age onwards, guiding and diversifying its flora and fauna within strict limits, being myself guided and maybe diversified by it; and discovering where this relationship might lead.

So we must a walk little round it, in truly fresh air. And round the seasons as we do so, for they divide the year into comprehensible compartments along our path. We can only see a very little, but it should be varied. Natural history as much as gardening; silviculture and ecology as much as design; and impressions of scent and colour, texture and light, rarefied – refined if you will – beneath a cool northern sky.

> *No flab*
> *in this landscape. No cushion*
> *for the bones. Just muscle.*
> *And the fat*
> *packed tight*
>
> *into corners*
> *for the winter...* [9]

21

WINTER

It is logical to begin with winter. To come across it halfway interrupts the programme of growth; to end with it slams the door shut. We will set out from winter's first crystal, through spring and summer, to the ripeness of autumn.

Most years, winter begins by mid-November. Before this, snow would have lain on the hills, and frosts would have visited. But these were autumn frosts, whitening yellow foliage in early morning; and all day, through weak sunlight, leaves would have fallen as they thawed, a hesitant detachment from birch, a light clatter from hazels. Young ash suddenly one morning would have cast the lot: lying in a black dropped armful about their ankles. Incidents, portents of the change.

A winter frost is different. It is natural, expected. The sun is no longer on speaking terms. Change has arrived. Leaves are all down, creaking underfoot, and branches look the other way. Stems are frozen in their various attitudes; as a Welsh poet claimed some thousand years ago, in such weather

> ....*a man could stand on a single stalk.* [6]

There is a tang and freshness in the air, an elasticity. Lines are drawn clearer, rains have retreated, a cold buttoned-up discipline invigorates. Wallace Stevens noted that

> ....*After the leaves have fallen, we return*
> *To a plain sense of things.*

Such early days of winter therefore open the garden to searching inspection. Tree-form and proportion of evergreen stand bare, unassisted by autumn colour or spring promise; and before snow has arrived to bury or bend everything to its own purposes. So I survey the framework, resolve what trees would be better away, what new ones might be encouraged, and which sheltering evergreens are forgetting their role of backdrop to bright deciduous stems and twiggery.

These sunny snowless periods are beautiful as well as instructive. Species rhododendrons from the East, though useless for shelter, always catch the eye then; their limbs climb deliberately with neat thoughtful leaves, each species to its own tune, the heavier down in the deep bass of shady dells, the lighter rippling among sunlit woodwinds of birch and rowan.

I could fill pages with the delights of bole, bark and twigwork – the great bay-coloured haunches of Douglas fir, eminently slappable as you walk past them – it is early winter, they are docile, they have yet to bear the burden of snow and the leap of spring is far off; or the impeccably smooth gunmetal taper of American firs; birch saplings with stems of every shade through mahogany, copper, pink or whitewash-white (rub them with your sleeve and see), Nepalese species no better than those from down the road; snake-bark maples whose cream and olive stripes look too good to be true, painted as if by the *Douanier* Rousseau... Red and aromatically flaking trunks of Scots pine, black impressive ones of lodgepole pine; grey powerful Sitka spruce, now clear of its abrasive adolescent tangle... So many more. And, decorating deciduous twigs and branches, even some boles, the silvery ash-green filigree of lichens; in strands, embossment or overlacing drapery, sparkling after rain and adding always a fine-worked delicacy to the bare strength of trees.

Of evergreens, at any season, juniper pleases most. Miss Jekyll accurately and affectionately described its subtle vivacity, and the shorter bluer needles of our local race are always alert, the whole bush active in profile. But juniper has probably been here since the ice went back and is heir to 8,000 years of accumulated ills; our original 'elfin woodlands' of juniper have been decimated by snow, gale and disease. Fresh ones planted in the same place die (a common, inexplicable, horticultural happening) and I have searched the globe's offering of juniper lookalikes to reproduce those wiry drought-proof aspirations, eventually finding some that are fairly satisfactory, their billows passable at a distance.

The pleasure from form and texture is not marginal here, but curiously intense. One early December in hard frost I recorded that low sun lit the pines a brilliant glassy green, with bark 'red velvet against iron shadows'. It is the contrast that tells, for we don't enjoy the regular rich winter colours of low-country woodlands. We have delicate mosses of every shade of green and yellow, leaves of lime-green wood sorrel folded in shelter, the finely-stamped leather-green fronds of Hard fern, and the rather tired ochreous green of woodrush; but these are seen only in the intermittent thaw. When real cold comes, colour and contrast go under the snow, and all that cannot hide there is darkened to death or dormancy. Leaves darken with cold, different species at different temperatures, so I judge the cold from the change in leaves. Some, like those of Chinese rhododendrons, roll inwards too, to minimise freeze-drying, terrifyingly black below -12°C, utterly withdrawn, mineral not vegetable.

In great silent cold, below -20°C, big trees from the Northwest American coast begin to groan audibly. Roots, though, are safe beneath blankets of needles or turf, and the prisms, fans and daggers of ice only penetrate a short way down.

Snow, also, protects them. In late November we suffer, or enjoy, the first snowfall. There have been warnings over the previous couple of months, strays in the wind, mornings dusted white, a whole day white in cold shadow. But one afternoon

> *Out of the grey*
> *indicative east....* [9]

the wind will drop; a heaviness clouds the sky, apprehensive silence gathers. Then, a prickle on the skin. Then another, invisible in the suddenly damp air. Distant hills, nearer trees, grow paler; a breath of wind passes; and waves of snow reach us. The curtain falls in a crisp murmur of flakes, a quiet piling of crystals, swarming and endless. It has begun.

24

it is the great
adequacy:
and looks in through the kitchen window
while the bread is being cut.

beneath it
the lewd earth turns restlessly.
it will go away
but must come back because what else

is as white as snow or calls
with delicate immensity
to help us bury the summer?
treat it kindly. do not doubt it.

we would never be done without it. [1]

On average I tread snow somewhere in this garden for eighty-seven days in a year, sometimes over a hundred.

After the first light fall the picture is quite changed. Trees and bushes relax, anonymous, into landscape, absolved from fuss of vegetation. All is hushed, the silence an insulation from, not absence of, noise. There is a constant background hiss as airy cakes detach themselves, the slow following dust puffing against black trunks. A moderate snowfall is entirely a delight, it builds different high confectioneries on each kind of conifer; it canopies deciduous trees translucently against blue sky; it blows glitteringly about you from wind-stirred branches. Boots crump or sigh on dry powder, they discover new glades unprinted by foot. Everything is fresh, uncomplicated; work becomes minimal.

it is only the simple sunlight
on a fence post
out of the snow,

and I come to set it upright
at the cost
of a single blow.

then I leave them to the sunlight.
one straight post,
trodden snow. [1]

A heavy snowfall extinguishes complacency, obliterates horticulture. Southeast winds moan for a day or two and then unload suffocatingly for one, two or three days more. The result is a degree of havoc.

When shelter was precious, I waded about poling snow from the more brittle or stupid trees and shrubs, an endless task. As the fall increases, cumbered heads of even tall birches bow down, until by torchlight they become huge veils streaming underfoot, scarcely distinguishable from the blizzard itself. Tug after tug frees them, loosening avalanches on head and shoulders. Next morning young birches, struck by the pole, spring back gratifyingly through a shower of crystals – 'They're so proud, young trees'[10], remarked the Norwegian poet Olav Hauge after poling his own apple orchard – and birches never rise straight again if shamed by being held down for long by the hair; Robert Frost, you may remember, added further indignities. I saved many trees by poling, and destroyed some also; but the exercise was worth it, for nothing is worse than having to watch, from behind windows, the dismemberment of years.

I recall one morning when a great many trees had been shattered, and others were exploding in the stillness (for trees burst under stress). The air was acrid with birch juice. Huge chandeliers of ice, dizzy rotating glaciers twenty feet up, menaced progress. Light slanted through strange new spaces and snow-hung wreckage. It was dawn after the air raid. Landmarks had vanished, those lichened columns known and patted for years; no familiar space-measurers, no eye-intervals, were left. And as it was April, bird song thrilled through the devastation.

I remember such things with a kind of pleasure, looking at a wood now attractive in its fresh light, edged with the history of change. The memory cools sweaty Augusts. Years become incidents as we move with the garden, part of our four-dimensional landscape.

Birches are notorious for snow-break, because their closely-woven twigs clot together. Pines also, from their mat of needles, the long gangling limbs they never know what to do with, and their brittleness. These trees demand full light, and are doomed if shaded one side, as when bordering a wood; snow piles on the better-lit branchier aspect and sooner or later the whole goes over. Paradoxically, snow-break increases in the lee of a new shelterbelt; this creates a vacuum which attracts the diverted snow, and stout old birches there – having laid down their previous hundred and fifty annual rings among snow-dispersing winds – now find themselves unprepared to shoulder the load, and break down. One has to be careful, interfering.

Trees operate different strategies in snow. Exotic spruce and fir, used to this sort of thing, stand firmly at attention, arms to sides, slabbed almost vertically; a touch frees them of any load. Others, like scrub willows, bend low and rise with double-joints undamaged. But juniper collapses rigidly and suffers torture of the rack as frozen snow around it melts and refreezes, dragging it irresistibly down and fracturing bones. Yet juniper has survived such abuse for millions of years: cutting away injured limbs sometimes ensures a swarm of infant shoots on a bough apparently too venerable to consider such things; and the uninjured ones extend their spread.

when snow has lain
week after week,
been soldered down,
its ice will break

slowly, deliberately
branches. but lower
branches only.
branches higher

swing green till the next
snowfall. meanwhile
birds gobble blue berries in sunlight,
roots do their best
to be careful. [1]

After a blizzard there generally follow days of blue sky, often intensely cold. The snow lies in long fluted drifts, well over six feet in places, marble where wind has polished it, furred where loose grains are gathered, fashioned into familiar winter furnishing, subtly different every year. Whole areas have vanished, rough slopes smoothed to a huge iced cake, smaller shrubs invisible, larger ones blue-shadowed waves that hiss silkily beneath your skis.

I used to try and dig them out if small, or reach down and settle snow about them so they were at least buried upright in the heroic manner. The shovel uncovered successive laminations of snow surface, registers of storm before storm, and any surface formerly exposed during a thaw carried a dark speckling of birch seed and a scatter of folded insects, their flight over; you turned back the pages of winter. Deep down, dry snow loosened to sugar in water, great hollows opened under permeable crust, swallowing the slush, and I pushed in both arms and worked the branches free. After such obstetrics the more precious shrubs peered from holes surrounded by great snow heaps, erect again and bewildered; some of five feet high and across being found at the bottom of the pit pressed to eighteen inches, seemingly flat and extinct as *Archaeopteryx*. They flowered that summer. Sometimes broken twigs from the wreckage were saved as cuttings, and I possess several healthy bushes born in that Caesarian fashion.

But I and my plants are now too old for this sort of thing. It is better to accept the snow, enjoy it, put on skis for the hill or – if the surface hardens – to explore on foot.

> *Raspberry bramble nettle*
> *great field thistle.*
> *Even dwarf willow.*
>
> *In summer*
> *quite intractable.*
> *You can't get through.*
>
> *You wait for the snow.*
> *Snow smooths everything level.*
> *Is above all argument.*
>
> *Then you walk straight on*
> *hear the stems crackle*
> *leave footprints for the moon.* [9]

One morning the cold will hesitate, the afternoon be milder, with a southwest wind. You hear – a dripping: astonishing sound... Eagerly, boughs slip to blackness, twigs shiver and plop their load, winter sluices trunk to trunk. More wonderful still, the thaw continues overnight, snow watering off needles, and the naked trees grinning at you by torchlight. Everyone exults. Next morning wakes to damp monochrome, the snow deadened and its greyness under tree-drip pitted with eyes. Plants stretch audibly, the taller junipers sighing, pushing back their coffin lids, shaking free clots of cold jelly, and springing up black and spiry again, beaded with water. Competent firs and spruce slip off shoulder burdens and resume photosynthesis; pines emerge sheepishly, stiff with cramp, needles jammed together, pulled out of bed without warning. The sudden dark vertical of these conifers startles against that long-familiar flat white. Even a little turf is bared, most gentle of carpets now, velvet slippers. But hills are still wintry. The thaw is local.

> *a black wind*
> *has cleared the snow.*
> *the ground*
> *sobs and is soft again, go*
>
> *higher and find*
> *eight months frost.*
> *wind*
> *white and faithful to the last.* [1]

And soon all stiffens again; clear skies return. I tidy broken trees, sometimes huge ones toppled over. Pleasant, yellow saw-dust trodden into snow, April-smelling boughs stacked in sun, blue smoke from an orange chain-saw drifting across white glades. Pleasant; for efficient surgery is satisfying, and I no longer need every cubic inch of timber to fight the wind. I can relax, gaze around.

> *enough spruce*
> *cut this winter,*
> *enough ice*
> *and crushed needles,*
> *air*
> *biting with resin,*
> *yellow bruise*
> *on snowglare.*
> *enough that's brilliant,*
> *saw-tooth. what else*
> *on offer?*
>
> *I pause*
> *join deft flit*
> *of a robin*
> *about piled branches,*

wary of stem-juice;
on the lookout
for rare softness,
something of use. [1]

Not only snow but ice furnishes our winter garden. That little mountain river, the Burn, can become exciting even though it disappears blankly for long periods. I once had to keep a short stretch of it unfrozen – or at least impassable with ice ditches. It taught me a good deal.

Despite the school books, swift water does not freeze from the top downwards; but from the sides, and from the bottom upwards. Below -8°C air temperature, long crystals assemble there, much of the bed growing gelid with spongy ice, and splashed stones above carry all textures of ice known to a winter climber, from brittle to rubbery.

Waterfalls and rapids swell with these accumulations, deeper water skins with more ice, which is added also, so that the river builds up higher than its banks. Water level fluctuates violently. Temporary ice-dams downstream raise it high, choke the flow, and the surface freezes. Then the dam is dislodged, water sinks and the now hollow surface sags and breaks to leave successive jagged rims round banks and boulders – most treacherous to cross, on two legs or four.

This winter Burn in a cold spell, then, becomes a chain of roaring yellow gushets, trunked and frozen falls, and remote blue caverns. A chilly place to garden in; when 'ditching' I often had to chip spade or mattock free of fresh ice every few minutes. It made pleasant memories beside the fire that evening; and by scented Himalayan primulas at the same spot a few months later.

A thaw brings dramatic relief. You hear the bolts drawing back. Honey-coloured floods pour out, tilt up the ice sheets, sweep across them and bellow through all those collapsing grottoes. Bobbing and spinning, the debris thunders downstream;

from the bridge, as compulsive to watch as the hypnotic wake of an icebreaker. You share the catharsis.

The upper part of the arctic Gorge is hard to reach even before a thaw drowns it, requiring alpinist techniques and a degree of optimism. Cliffs rise around you fluted with organ pipes of icicles, stalactites and stalagmites, thigh-thick; and the waterfall, that aesthetic climax at other seasons, becomes a muscular one, its 35-foot ice pitch demanding axe and crampons; the edge of any success sharpened by potential drops on to ice-stakes or the thin lid of a cauldron.

More leisurely inspection of the Burn reveals that an otter has passed that way. Its broad heavy paw marks and wallow of tail clamber into and out of horrendous gashes in the ice, and a bloody mix of snow and scales, maybe a trout head, indicate a meal. Mink tracks, smaller and neater, and dancing prints of water vole, elaborate the otter's perambulation.

For snow reveals who shares this garden with me. Animals and birds quickly sign on. I follow their tracks avidly, as some substitute for those radio-waves of scent all about us that we can never tune into.

Outside the fence runs a furrow beaten brown by uncountable small feet from distant burrows, peppered with a grapeshot of droppings. One grim day I see these tracks, chilling as any Crusoe found, impudently casual – *inside*; and heart-sinking balls of dung. Rabbit... Then it is a hunt, by torchlight if necessary, before the intruder has time to lay false trails, so that his entry can be found and blocked. Then, emergency; for until he is caught, nothing is safe. In early days with less cover about, I used to pursue him myself. Now I rely principally upon Staff Cats, lofty professionals who disdain the laity's evidence of visible tracks, and conduct their own – often nerve-wrackingly prolonged – investigations along official lines of scent. Invariably successful, they do not share my anxiety. A hungry rabbit eats virtually anything vegetable, and in snow rings round and kills tall young trees. Rabbits create deserts; I have watched the astonishing regeneration on nearby hills during the myxomatosis years – and the desolation before, and since.

> *we leave boot*
> *prints, paw*
> *prints in the snow, to-fro*
> *round about*
> *the new green spruces, hop*
> *here to there, stop*
> *scrape and peer, go on –*
> *to where? we lead a criss-*
> *cross chase, each one*
> *alone beneath the high*
> *unmelting sun.*
> *he with his teeth, I*
> *with my gun.* [1]

Red squirrel tracks in wet snow alarmingly resemble those of small rabbits but, explicably, vanish into thin air before a tree. During long cold anticyclones when snow does not melt nor wind blow, the surface is tinily staccatoed by mouse feet – plus flick of tail – and clumsily oared by voles. These colleagues of mine compete with each other and myself – voles by day, mice by night, both shifts dawn and dusk – all year round and in winter through long tunnels under the snow from plant to plant. More purposeful dimplings of weasels and stoats, politically correct, are rarer because cats – whose logic is not mine – devour their owners as readily as if they were voles or rabbits.

Bird feet, too. From aggressive hop of blackbird to portly stroll of cock pheasant, attended by weighty tail; woodcock, shorter, stubbier, more nervous; blackcock, swaggering; and small birds, bad when delighting with me in buds, good if not. My relations with those fellow beings queuing behind us at the evolutionary fruit machine and – so far – not receptive of higher instructions, are mixed. Especially in a severe winter.

birds present the problem
in its most immediate form.

pipelegs, feathers,
whisper of breath

cocked eye and beak;
underneath,

a puffed throat
imminence of note

unbearable. dismiss them.
they can whistle

elsewhere. birds
are a quick urge

of greed and seasons.
for these reasons

deserve respect.
tamed, are abject

flutterers to be despised.
I cannot understand

why I am pleased
when they feed from my hand. [2]

And so this season passes. Snow diminishes, or returns less often, and green snouts push through last year's drying leaves. But spring waits for the next chapter. It has begun to snow again, and winter is still with us, filling in its vista of year by year repetition, as if to persuade us of a sufficiency beyond our one visit.

No, it is not repeat
repeat, it is once
only and enough.

These juniper berries bunched,
sun-bosomed through the frost-
needles in the bright

snow-light meet their first
chance to last next
spring, and no more;

rounded-off tough
sky-blue bloomed, their green
one-year behind

successors crowding about them.
It is enough
to have seen a stiff

laden juniper branch
pausing as you are
passing, just now once

out of the snow and never,
coming back how often,
to see it this way again.

The prize, the primacy of it
the instantaneous thousand
cold needles ever

afire and berries
thrusting their one spring
aware out of the cluster. [4]

SPRING

I feel the first hint of spring here some day in early March: the delicious wet scent of sun-dry grass in melting snow, or the tang of birch buds on a damp evening. But spring really arrives, well wrapped up, about the end of that month, and a good place to welcome it is the south-facing slope of the pine wood, above the Gorge, where against the blue snowy gloom opposite I can watch pine buds in the sun swell to gold, the first flush of rising life. Or any other turfy bank when sap begins to move all round you and overflows sparkling from broken birches; when bees crowd snowdrops, bronze flies stud boulders, and small awakened beetles run up and down the straws of last year's grass. Or by the Pool – across its melting surface pondskaters scuttle to warm themselves on stones that tilt south; and the surrounding mud murmurs with frogs.

At this time, along what Wallace Stevens would call the 'slim radiance' of hazel alleys, hazel catkins, clenched all winter, let themselves down, golden and heraldic. We once possessed a huge oak-like goat sallow that every March purred with an umbrella of silver ones, later opening to yellow: then the tree filled to a vast hive of bees audible far off on still mornings, celebrating a private spring. Catkins against blue sky rightfully decorate a marginal garden at this season.

But wind determines our spring. For example, a southwesterly hastens it. Then I sit in the sun and watch the snow edging darkly to water, its drops running together and disappearing, and the old land emerging from beneath; islands fusing to peninsulas, peninsulas flooding to great insect-stirring continents... until only a few wet crystals and a damp stain are left on the flattened white stalks.

East wind calls back winter overnight, with knee-deep drifts; the prevailing north, northwesterly and northeasterlies carry flurries of snow, strung mists of it processing down the glen. As these winds can continue through May into early June, blowing bitter from snowfields above, shelter is essential here.

At the start, shelter did not exist. Thin unclad scrub funnelled and infuriated the blast for weeks on end; dry leaves battered about and dead stems complained, night and day. Nothing is so tiring as continual wind. There is nowhere to rest.

Brief intervals in such gales bring a stunned silence, almost a giddiness, like stepping ashore after a rough crossing. In early days I could only kick aside fallen twigs and wait for the next storm to roar across Druim Albainn, the bare backbone of Scotland and our unchecked horizon.

Even today I can revisit those stark years by venturing to our new – 3-foot high – shelterbelts outside the garden proper: there again to fight flattening exposure while a dozen yards away branches stir lightly behind their 35 years of painfully built-up shelter. Now, an important part of this horticultural kind of exploration is the frankly scientific noting what species or races of a species resist the punishment of such a site: the usual books and articles record irritatingly little, and that suspiciously similar in all. Cold and wind are only two of the testing factors; others include shade, acidity, nutriment, water and physical damage. A successful species balances contentedly in equilibrium between its received stresses and the strategies – external and internal – it has evolved to overcome them. Internal, too, for – to take an example – just as externally the relative positioning of a leaf in shade is cunningly arranged to receive optimal sunlight, it possesses internally a molecular photochemical system built, stocked and tuned to give maximal efficiency for whatever intensity of light its position exposes it to. So as well as visible morphological adaptations to suit the shade, wind, frost or other stresses of an environmental niche, there exists – not unexpectedly – a whole series, and series of series, of modifications far below the visible; these subtle changes being tied efficiently into the energy budget of the whole plant by alterations in other working molecules. We therefore expose vistas of 'molecular ecology' – only detectable by laboratory techniques – underlying the one we see. The pleasure of discovering and mentally fingering such things is endless, and to learn even a little about them – without ever trying to cultivate the refractory margins of Chance or Causality – adds to the fascination of a site like this, and tempers the spring blast we suffer from.

I employ many devices against such a wind. 'Straightforward' shelterbelts of course; but no shelterbelt of any interest (or efficiency) is straightforward. You have to consider rate of growth, shade tolerance, matters like that, and keep it furnished from top of dominant trees to ground cover. By selective thinning, discussed under Autumn, I ensure sufficient light for a varied understorey against winds rushing past the bare legs of taller trees, which raise their skirts as they grow. This understorey contains shade-bearing trees and shrubs, some sheared back, 'bushed', for closer texture; many being deciduous to lighten the picture and blend restfully.

In more open places, not facing north, I baffle the wind with informal 'hedges' or grouped bushes. These are clipped – 'moulded' in the Japanese fashion – to flow into their immediate landscape like receding planes of scenery on a stage, sliding first from one side, then the other. They check wind, help to make garden compartments, and reduce frost build-up by assisting drainage of cold air. Such bonsai landscaping builds perspectives without you waiting three generations to see them, or bankrupting two in the process.

This touching-up of walls, doorways, even vaulting, of the garden compartments is almost compulsive. Your tools are ladder, saw, secateurs and shears, and you must be careful both horticulturally and artistically for, as in other kinds of wood-engraving, what you take out you can't put back. I check myself and only barber a tiny proportion of trees and bushes, to let the others show off their colour, form and movement without distraction. Otherwise, the common disaster of suburban culture.

> ... look at the wild birch.
> and then what you have done.
> with your sly touch,
> your knife's edge,
> to make it fit
> under your sun, sit
>
> in your hedge,
> inhabit
> your street. to make it sweat
> through that clean cut
> all last night such hate, white
> from the root. [2]

Frost hazard in spring can be reduced otherwise than by air drainage. A militant 70-foot group of Sitka spruce at one corner, bastion against climatic assault, began thirty-four years ago as 1-foot infants regularly cossetted on cold evenings with woolly nightcaps twisted round their leading shoots, removed each morning; without these, they would still be knee-high, like decades-old dwarfs in frost hollows throughout commercial plantings. Precious East Asian rhododendrons wore dabs of dry turf, sheets of polythene netting, or even a golf umbrella; one, known as the Elephant because of its great pachyderm ears, bore a howdah of pine clippings.[11] The danger is not to blossoms or shoots, which regenerate, but to boughs flushing with spring sap; on freezing, these may split. If winds dry out the split, whole branches die; so I tape injuries firmly, and many healthy survivors bear fragments of bandage from battles long ago. Frost strikes suddenly, whenever night clouds dissolve.

out of a clear sky
comes frost the killer
ending the spring, wounding the summer.
we have new leaves for autumn
but by then
the sun is one of the stars again. [1]

When you garden an edge, it can cut sharply. I tell how bad a late frost has been, from the damage to emerging sensitives like Lady fern; or bracken, whose fronds map out a frost hollow, remaining green above it, progressively wilting from yellow to brown to black as they descend the pit.

But all about us, plants are stirring, flowers preparing. As W.C. Williams noted,

> *....the profound change*
> *has come upon them; rooted, they*
> *grip down and begin to awaken...*

The principal delight of a garden is wandering round it; and in spring watching eyes open. This book cannot be a horticultural account, so we are excused pages of character studies of these multiform creatures as they appear, unbutton, take leaf, flower, fruit and depart; we keep to the overall view, with chosen examples, and merely note shoots crimson and plump, cold and pale green, rising sinisterly from cobra coils, or stretching invitingly like the white arms of sweet cicely. They have begun to move; nothing can stop them,

> *.... even a mushroom*
> *will break up a pavement.* [4]

The earliest spring flowers – snowflake, snowdrop, red lungwort, coltsfoot, barren strawberry – thrive in appropriate areas for dry or damp, sun or shade, each so fitted for its niche it mixes perfectly with its fellows there; such as, say, lesser celandine in streams and pools of shining yellow, simple and satisfying, lingering on through wood anemone into days of primroses, violets and cuckoo flower and, like them, indispensable to the rich mosaic of spring floors.

These natives flower where they will. Planted primroses die out, but those natural to a damp sunny spot above the Gorge appear each spring as snow departs, like stars in a clearing sky. They flourished there before the spruce were planted; as the trees grew they flowered around them; now the tall spruce are gone and burnt up the chimney they still flower there, clumped among white tussocks of grass. Again, wood anemones are spring showpieces that flood the garden, acres of them, running through hazel and birch, clambering about the banks of the Burn, washing against drifts of blue pulmonarias and dazzling in sheets below the taller woods. These and other spring flowers are helped to remain and spread by various techniques; and if, as often, they insist on moving, are ushered along, encouraged, by pulling out surrounding competitors or disabling these with careful herbicide. I have greatly increased our wild flowers by such marginal gardening; and visitors obligingly assume the plants have done it all by themselves.

Daffodils are among our earliest imports to bloom. Many are small cupped kinds of subtle shade and presentation, all rising from moss or woodland leaves. I try to arrange them suitably: groups of milk-white and lemon under rusty-barked pine, for instance, and the more stolid next to equally uncompromising boulders; fresh bicolors drift in crescents up a wide birch-clad bowl, crowding the side-chapels there and culminating about a semicircle of flowering currant: three increasingly airy storeys of colour and texture – daffodils, delicately fountaining shrubs in palest pink, and a green mist of unfolding larch needles. Elsewhere, daffodil clumps rhyme with similarly radiating fans of hazels, glinting in the sun together. They are kindly flowers, domestic, asking to be picked for invalids.

> *he named the unknown mountain, now*
> *its frost*
> *takes care of the east. out*
> *in a deckchair wrapped in a rug*
> *he savours new zeros. his*
> *grandchildren tiptoe past. spring has begun.*
> *the daffodils they brought him*
> *crisp in a jug*
> *untwist, take flower,*
>
> *melt green in the sun.* [1]

These blossoms, and myriads more, awaken the garden. They should be imagined in a setting of just-leafing birches and about-to-unfurl hazels, of tall poplars sticky with scent, all trees tense, sap driving up them; of thickets shrill with bird song and wide glades bright with the first insects. Flowers, as always here, are a welcome extra, but never essential to any season. In some Japanese gardens a flower might well embarrass the chaste design, but this framework is robust enough to take armfuls of them; provided of course that they 'fit' – and we shall come to that later.

Young birches leap emerald among black spires of juniper and the sober exuberance of hazels; yet spring foliage of every tree is joyous, through dusty white of aspen, sulphur yellow of red oak, that almost blinding green of larch to the velvety copper of amelanchier. It rivals the kaleidoscopic understorey of flowers. A feast not only for the eye. Fences, of unrelaxing intent, must be secure.

The besieging innocent
graze nearer.
Implacable deer
intractable rabbit.
They will devour.

Lord of fresh leaves
your estate does you credit.
They started the war.
You must exhibit
imperial habit

do not despair.
Tighten the wire.
Stand by your gun.
Especially in spring
cherish iron.

That is what
empire's about.
Six hectares of crop
coming up
for redistribution. [9]

Of my own crop, azaleas and rhododendrons are notable, for quite a few withstand our cold dry climate. Among heather and blaeberry the small-flowered alpine kinds of Europe and Asia appear almost native. So does the taller common yellow azalea.[12] No blossomer of its intensity runs so well with natural vegetation, from its winter thrust and twigginess, the readiness of its vigorous leaves to fill up holes, and the sheer vivacity of its ever-delicate flowers. It punctuates hazels, blows among heather, shines along woodland corridors, always full of gladness and never putting anyone else to shame. Other azalea species, white, cream, pale pink, accompany it through spring woodland, with triflora rhododendrons – white, pink, lilac – equally open and slender-leaved, lightly sun-dappled among awakening oak and rowan stems or wind-silvery against Scots pine; and all above that surf of wild flowers.

Along the Dell axis, these strings give way to the bass – or the large trumpets. Here the big-leaved Himalayan rhododendrons dwell, curtained by bamboo, hemlock and hazel, safe from tempest. The Dell winds between water-worn low cliffs that broaden occasionally into bowls of sunlight. Mossy paths and lawns replace the vanished post-glacial river, flowing through successive intimate rooms where rocky banks swing out and in as you enter and leave, and tall trees meet overhead at the narrows.

Near the top of this little glen flowers a hugely dignified 12-footer, wide as high; its corollas unfold exquisite and enormous, blush paling to opalescent crystal-white with green-speckled throat; unfrosted, they last, with haunting scent, a full month.[13] Yet this uncompromising exotic looks astonishingly 'right' in this place at this time: all its splendid improbability swept up in the zest of a northern spring and no more unexpected than the surrounding excitement of shrill birch and hazel shoots, where for months (it seemed for ever) had been frost, snow and broken branches.

Others, lower down the Dell, float their crimson-throated primrose trusses among glaucous foliage and effortless branch-work; or climb with soft pink bells, sparkling after rain, through tiers of blue-green leaves, pure blue shoots jostling the deeper pink unopened flowers. Species rhododendrons like these, rising from memorably blue Himalayan poppies beneath hanging streamers of tall laburnum, blend imperturbably with surrounding native vegetation, remarkably generous of flower yet never crowded or gross. With coarser blooms, such a localised outbreak of colour could disturb a garden like this.

For example, the Dell also houses, or stables, a few 'hardy hybrid' rhododendrons. Its aqueous shade slims their cabbagey proportions to a degree of deportment. When assisted by sympathetically unrolling ferns and lacy umbellifers, they achieve distinction at a distance, hoarse colours softened and weighty blooms persuaded apart, the Brassica tendency overcome. But close at hand they pant in your face; you bless the maidenly composure of native woodruff when sidling past their frilly solicitations.

That kind of plant is just not suitable for the Dell, or easy to place anywhere here. Its uncorseted truss and sprawling branchery have obviously been 'planted'. Its flowering is certainly an event, but must be led up to by other blossoms; by itself it detonates. And choosing the other blossoms so that they are not so elegant they vulgarise the hybrid further, or raucous enough themselves to join in the Big Bang, I find difficult. Hardy hybrids are best kept to white and cool colours, well diluted among woodland, in this place. Elsewhere of course, they can be impressive dowagers, triumphs of High Victorian, Imperial Edwardian, taste. One needs considerable phytosociological tact in gardening.

Up in sun and wind, bright among junipers, blow the clean simple spring roses; but roses are mostly summer plants and I deal with them later. Let us close with a brief – as usual, a frustratingly brief – mention of some animals of spring, that bustling, burrowing, straw-packing, twig-collecting throng and, of them, largely – to remain as objectively subjective as I can – those whose activities if uncontrolled would defeat or greatly retard the parallel and equally worthy ones of the gardener.

An emotive subject. Marginal gardening here depends on shelter. Deer – which lethally fray young tree stems and bite off leading shoots – and rabbits can both be kept out by a galvanised-iron curtain, but mice and voles run freely about; and one vole with mind and stomach to it can girdle and kill a hundred young trees within a week. If trapping house mice can be allowed, so must that of field mice. Also, I have proved to myself that much destruction starts as fashions, crazes: such as biting off – not eating – the emergent noses of Solomon's seal and stacking them at burrow entrances for neighbours to admire. Some local entrepreneur is responsible; his companions become addicted; bereaved stems sob helplessly around them. If I trap the activists at once, the habit does not spread, and vole tradition is spared that particularly self-destructive individual talent. Compared with loss of shelter, amputation of Solomon's seals is mere annoyance, and readily stopped with least violence to voles. I keep retaliatory measures to such a minimum; otherwise both 'pest' and gardener suffer, the latter becoming prosecutor, judge, jury and hardened executioner or humbug. So I turn away when hooligan blackbirds tear up moss lawns and drive back discomfited cats every spring; but do not lament overmuch when fewer return after a severe season. Their numbers soon recover.

> *a bitter winter it has been.*
> *just three birds left.*
> *they preen in the sun, they whistle, do not seem*
> *bereft.*
>
> *last year is over, that cock thrush*
> *treads it beneath.*
> *he's two new wives to choose from, and will use*
> *them both.* [2]

Direct assault on your aesthetic crop is more provoking. Wild cherry blossom is sometimes stripped by bullfinches fired with spring. The gardener, likewise stimulated by warming blood, is tempted to equal excess. This recurrent dilemma of humanity is summarised below, under the title 'Joy'. Do I distance myself from it by explaining that Japanese cherries will not grow here?

Twenty seven bullfinches
in one week
of sun

visited the blossom –
so sparse
now the years

close in – of my cherry trees
from Japan. They enjoyed
each opening bud

as much as I did, not
for the whiteness
not for food

but the delight
of ripping them out
and throwing them down, a circle of white

distressing the grass
under each tree. Pure
anarchy, sheer

destruction. There was something about them
misusing the sun
for private joy

that offended my sense
of our common inheritance. And must have been why
each day, I shot them.

Twentyseven bullfinches
in one week of sun. The best,
almost, with that particular gun. [4]

SUMMER

Summer unfolds, spreads into an upholstery of foliage. Leaves lie back, drink the lazy sun; flowers relax. The sense of urgency has left garden and gardener. Summer birches silver with wind along every ridge, their mature leaves glossy, twigs polished. Birch foliage flickers with a million points of light even on a calm day. As background, it suits our small scale. Any coarser foliage so abundant so high would squeeze the place in; we would suffocate. It is buttressed below by rough matt hazel leaves, solidly down to earth; these two trees partner each other round the garden and the seasons, a living framework. In the high summer sea of birch, leaves of other trees – every species with its own colour and movement – create eddies and islands. Young sessile oak, for instance, richer and choppier than birch, but with leaves multilobulate enough to keep the scale; or those of hornbeam, that successful import, delicately translucent and following only a little less pliably the flutter of birch, multiplying the shadows of their ribbed venation. Natural features are outlined in foliage now: the hidden Gorge by dark alders and pale ash; above them, sunlit white aspens and blue-bottled pine; in shadow opposite, crags spiring with conifers and determined rowan.

All this expanding Paradise – Lower Paradise – tends to engulf the structure of the place; its compartments become stuffed with flowers and confused by foliage. Yet we are so topographically complex we must keep the overall plan visible; otherwise, rather than surprise, it bewilders – delightful in detail but overwhelming in the mass. An unorganised profusion.

To restore calm, other reassurances, other clear verticals and horizontals must replace the obscured tree boles and distant perspectives. Our summer horizontals are the welcome flat – or fairly flat – grassy areas, as reassuring to meet on broken steep ground like this as sheets of water in more conventional gardens; our vertical points of reference are cleanly-contrasting bushes, round or pointed, and tall perennials, all appearing accidentally inevitable at strategic places. Mowing the lawns and trimming the verticals ensure they maintain this sense of order.

For example, our summer roses, mostly species, romp freely above their herbaceous attendants; and so they should, for a clipped wild rose is a pinioned bird. But they brandish their flowers about a dark vertical semi-formality of juniper, mountain pine, holly and beech bushes and are separated into the positions of their dance by alleys of well-shaven turf, the horizontal stabiliser of the plan.

I can hardly overstress the importance of this closely-mown green horizontal of lawns and paths. Even two inches' growth blurs the picture, unties its repose; the view of course may still be of interest, but one no longer in a garden. I minimise the little labour required by encouraging lawns and paths of moss, heath bedstraw or golden saxifrage, and using light Scandinavian hand-mowers for the grass, each kept in its own hut on its own axis. Frank lawns are small; others mere suggestions in bowls where only a path winding through and enlarging the base to a pocket-handkerchief sward needs mowing. The eye is satisfied by the neat pathway, and planting directs it there, so the sides of the bowl can carry longer grass, occasionally clipped or trimmed with a strimmer and, where it meets the shaven areas, graded by tilting the mower on one wheel, which appears to broaden the path and enlarge the lawn.

I shun motorised assistance as far as I can although, as in power-sawing or periodically strimming large stretches, it becomes at times essential. Not only is heavy machinery impracticable on steep rocky terrain, but its noise and fumes and maintenance obstruct one's partnership with the living garden. For trimming

49

round wild flowers in grass, the selective swing of long-han-
dled shears is safer; and mowing and clipping – never more than
two or three hours a week at high season – is a considerable satisfaction in gardening, and gardening is a major contribution to
enjoying a garden, not to be thoughtlessly delegated to bangs
and smoke, lengths of lethal cable, or hired men.

I discussed clipping verticals earlier. Of the unclippable verticals I must mention giant hogweed.[14] I arrange for this to rise
in important places and toast the summer. It towers on a single
stem to 14 feet, carrying three or four shorter declamatory arms
on the way up. The huge radar bowls of its umbels stare at the
sun through a Heathrow of bluebottles. Not beautiful; but nothing can rival its sudden structural power, and singly or in groups
it dominates its landscape, clinching what the others have to say.
Its leaves grumble for many years, elbowing over neighbours;
annually they swell larger on zoomorphically muscular stalks,
until one year the creature gathers all, takes a deep breath, and
launches upward. After that monumental gesture it persists in
standing though the table has long been cleared. You come
across it in autumn like a great gibbet peeled by the wind, and
its hollow ruin crackles underfoot many a season after; for flowering kills it. I know hogweed is preached against: it can pro-
voke unpleasant reactions in susceptible persons who embrace
it half-naked while sweating, and it poisons anyone who eats it
as rhubarb. Here, among reasonably normal people, it has been
an entertaining and harmless monster.

Other herbaceous verticals – lilies, aruncus, campanulas, in-
ulas, angelicas – accentuate the summer vistas, with foxgloves:
wild foxglove, not the buxom garden hybrid that looks as out
of place with us in summer as the equally smug Spanish blue-
bell does in spring beside the graceful native wild hyacinth –
not, alas, indigenous here. Certain other verticals explore
through the fence but, seeding vigorously, are firmly classed as
weeds, despite their unquestioned lineage.

...A tall docken
with a long stem
that rises from
the secret to the sun. [4]

Those native wild flowers not so classified – the vast majority – are satisfying, but infuriating. However skilfully I place my exotics I know I have imposed them on the indigenous community; whereas natives should be there anyway and my job is to persuade, not force, them into swathes and bands of coherent statement: very satisfying when successful. The infuriating part is finding that – while my back was turned – the natives have gone: vanished into carbon dioxide, or busy invading their neighbours.

So that in some turfy places introduced plants are the permanent occupants and the wild mosaic of fey unpredictable shifts around them year by year.

This wild mosaic blooms richest among the taller 'July Grass' of Richard Jefferies – hawkweeds, clovers, woundworts, umbellifers, buttercups, speedwells, more and more – rippling in a sea of purple and gold grass-heads: six or so weeks of enchantment and the rest of the year a rabble of stalks. I keep it strictly to a few small 'meadow' areas.

Yet, just to try and rule over these ephemerals can sometimes please better than more imperial gestures of gardening. You live like them, king for the day.

...of course it is
gratifying to see
those great cedars I planted,
evergreen
acres of them, such a fine
memorial, but in some ways

51

*I should like to die
clean.
annuals make
the best subjects.* [2]

Vertical or horizontal, wild or introduced, herbaceous plants
tie our roses down to their turf. Roses are not segregated, they
take their place with the rest, all year round, but only certain
shrub and species roses agree with our rather puritanical vegetation. They are mainly disposed, as I mentioned, among low
or bushed conifers such as junipers or pine, which march either
side and advance or retreat to make bays and centrepieces. Their
simple flowers strikingly illuminate this muted background of
needlework.

Dozens could be described, all fascinating creatures. I take
only two, that embody early summer, even spring, in their light-
someness, and typify roses here.

The earliest is an irrepressible species from Nepalese seed[15]
whose 12-foot arching stems carry, from May, hundreds –
thousands – of graceful ivory four-petalled flowers lustrous as
pearl. First blossoms are rather thin; when these wan frost-chil-
dren are over and the weather warms, the rest swarm into being. Foliage is equally light and precise, feathery leaflets among
translucent crimson thorns. By September it proffers multitudes
of scarlet heps, similarly elegant.

The second, a little later, is a Chinese mountain rose[16] whose
glorious single flowers – on different plants ranging from brick
red through scarlet to blood crimson, all with golden anthers –
are usually held far enough apart for their heraldic purity to be
savoured one by one; but sometimes every fountaining spray is
laden and the bush seems on fire, ferny foliage scarcely visible,
a remarkable sight above waves of wild white starwort and sa-
luted by tall blue lupins.

Roses here all bear single or semi-single flowers, white, cream,
yellow, blush, shell-pink, and again *gules* – velvety *gules* – and

52

or, of lank, creeping or sturdy habit; contrasting with conifer, turf and stone to bring out their freshness. Sometimes a red rose fades unhappily to blueish, or flaunts egregiously shining foliage; I cool it in the arms of a white one. Although sophisticated – High Tea – roses look hopelessly astray, party dresses among moorland, I indulge a few smouldering and astringently-scented half-wild cultivars in their own private arbours, attended by suitably sinister things out of Beardsley like monkshood, and circled with mildly deprecatory ferns.

Ferns are invaluable. When spring flowers die down and weedy grass is about to surge, ferns unroll to forestall it; by early summer they join tip to tip, green seas over. All reasonably permanent, ferns are our most useful low landscapers. We possess large stretches resembling the fern floor of New Zealand bush, covered, but not crowded, with quiet Quaker-like pertinacity of frond, neatly ordered as if planted there. Steep shady cliffs above the Gorge carry ferns patterned like tiles on a mediaeval roof, large fronds diminishing as they climb higher and drier to a ridgeline of tiny overlapping polypodys. The Gorge itself is a monsoon forest of ferns, mosses and liverworts, its overhanging walls cusped and vaulted to dripping aumbries and piscinas, cushioned wrist-deep in mysterious offerings.

One fern, bracken, increasingly dominates later summer. At first I thought it a weed and cut it back each July, quickly killing it, only to meet invading hordes of willowherb, wild raspberry and earthnut. Bracken keeps out these real weeds and can be harvested – without robbing its rhizomes of their year's food – in late summer, to provide useful mulch. But I leave most of it, for all summer and autumn its tabular fronds soothe great areas, their receding horizontals adding distance beneath birch trunks, richly contrasting with mown grass. You can practice miniature landscaping, with shears, on bracken in turf; winter wipes clean the mistakes.

I keep a slope of it pure, as a shoulder-high wilderness, a gentle sea of lapping fronds, skimming with brilliant insects. Lying down, you peer into subaqueous recesses, jade-green stems repeating infinitely, a convenient – though poverty-stricken – terrestrial substitute for

> *...the bubbled alleys, the reds*
> *and greens and purples,*
> *all those jewels...* [2]

of the underwater forests off the West Coast. But you at least hear things in this one – rustlings, cracklings, squeaks and pattering of busy unseen feet. It is their own jungle.

Bracken resists drought, drinking from deep rhizomes. Drought is our biggest summer constraint, like cold in winter or wind in spring. With sixteen hours of direct daily sun, the stony terraces of eastern glens, baked by hot winds from miles of blistering hill, can be as arid as anywhere in these islands. So much of my ground being rocky tors crammed with tree roots and bottomed by old glacier rubble, it soon dries up.

Just as you forecast snow or rain, you know when a drought is beginning. The last shower switched off halfway, a fortnight ago. Since then, gauzy clouds have scoured the sky from all directions, all rainless. Air is brassily unforgiving, winds search deep through cavities and vole tunnels until the ground shrinks, rocks and trees rising out of it, roots clutching dust. A north wind dries one side of a ridge while sun roasts the other and, the garden being a succession of ridges, not surprisingly after ten days or so plants become uneasy.

Smaller ones close down successively in a time-honoured sequence, and grass lies limp with a curious dull shine. Soil beside the Burn warms to crumbs, unwettable, and moss hardens. Tree foliage fades grey, grows harsh, and sometimes from site or genetics, shifts for safety into a precocious autumn, yellow leaves rattling down; but as long as buds stay plump all is well.

Old conifer needles fall faster, with thumps of cone, and soon even new ones of spruce turn pale and drop off, retreating higher up the trunk. Those trees from the wet west coast of North America stand stiff and preoccupied, and I tread tactfully about them; squirrels whisper above in worried committee.

Week after week of such weather is trying, and I prefer the company then of proven xerophytes, confident in aromatic wax. But for myself and the others, drought continues, thin clouds forage through dusty blue, thicker ones gather and disperse again. No rain comes, or ever will. There is an uncomfortable smell of death.

> ...*a garden*
> *has not courage to be desert.* [1]

I don't wait for the lights to go out. I water. I have to water, because of fire hazard. Heath and forest fires flourish around us at such times, the sun blood-orange for days through peaty smoke.

The Burn, that obvious source, has never yet run dry, but grows uncannily silent, as if it had vanished downstream. No movement, when you go to make sure, just an ominous string of pools, white stones, black seepage. Strands of algae, lured by warmth, bleach scabbily on unemployed rocks.

Sprinklers run from the Burn to susceptible areas, but a powerful fire pump damps down near the house. It drives sixty gallons a minute through an intestine of yellow hose to a weighty professional brass nozzle. Wielding that evocative instrument is exhilarating. Gallons, limitless hundreds of gallons, burst among dust and straining branches, cascade off foliage and stampede leaves and twigs before you along the paths. You recreate life at the twist of a nozzle. Frogs appear from nowhere, skipping underfoot like small wet ghosts; toads, less volatile beings, clamber with suppressed excitement. The jet drenches hemlocks back to the sunlit mists of Washington State. But it only dampens part of the garden; you smell the dried-up frontier in the dark.

Every drought ends, and the end almost justifies it. One evening the wind stops. Clouds lower; the air chills. Then, drops begin to tap on great yearning waterside leaves; a long-awaited sound, accompanied everywhere by black and shining spots ... They prick circles on pools; hiss faster and faster. Until a dull, liquid, releasing roar proclaims the unbelievable. A luxury to sit out in it, and soak.

Everything eases to life again. Moss blinks, raises its arms; leaves shake themselves like awakening dogs. All vegetation sits up and resumes business. Stones in the Burn darken, and water curls, then splashes, about them. The pump is lifted to the bank; no more hoses are unrolled. They are not yet rolled up.

Droughts apart, work in late summer is even more minimal, and it is pleasant to visit the heather plateau above the Burn. To get there one could scale the Gorge cliffs by a moderately difficult rock climb, best after fine weather has honed it to a purely private Artefact of Commitment:

> *a day to try*
> *the route direct, those crags collect*
>
> *no thunder, sky*
> *nothing but blue, no gods to crack*
>
> *that clean white rock, no winds to cry*
> *about its sharpness, no one by*
>
> *to check how near the top*
> *he who set it up*
>
> *climbs with delicate hands*
> *gap to gap*
>
> *glad of the almost absence.* [2]

Once there, I lounge about, idly misidentifying the glossy leaves, woolly muzzles or waxy bells of various moorland berry shrubs and wintergreens. Yet the main attraction is heather.[17] Heather erupts all over the garden in sunny places, and on turf with devil's-bit scabious sounds a pleasing major to the earlier minor of harebell and heath. But the plateau holds a bumpily level acre of it quite pure among rocks, a landscape in itself, maintained by clipping small areas at a time and removing stray tree seedlings; for heather is not a climax species here and after some twenty years of growing lankier would fall apart to let the next ecosystem develop. I prefer to keep my heather. This is a garden.

It opens barrage fitfully, some areas or strains glowing into flower before the mass. That tuning-up is a pleasant time to stroll the mounds and valleys up there in the sun. Underfoot, wandering strands of stagshorn clubmoss explore cracked peat, and lizards flash by or shimmer among lichens tipped scarlet like match-heads. It seems a long way from the rest of the garden.

Cultivated heathers are often more striking than soothing, yet wild heather here stays restful even in full bloom, not only because of the different colours – from deep purple to silver-lavender – and different stages of flowering that run across it like waves, but also from the sheer extent of satisfying texture washing against rock. I am grateful just to maintain this plateau, and frame it suitably with pine. No temptation to meddle.

We can shift axes and descend into the hidden Gorge. There I used to spend much time at the Burn itself, exploring under that clear amber water.[18] Maybe out in the current, clinging against its gale like the scuttling aquatic larvae about me, and seeing sunlight pattern itself across the pebble mosaic in every tint of yellow and gold beneath the travelling silver surface; ever in a stream of noise – rattling of bubbles, and the flat echo of some odd dislodged stone, measuring its one length nearer the sea. Or by a waterfall in a deep pool, visible afar through purple luminescence as a swinging cluster of glass beads; in relative calm and silence I curled against experienced bedrock and watched that perpetual dance of bubbles, beating and throbbing, an occasional leaf or twig in bewildered trajectory through them. Or right beneath the fall, fighting into its drenching uproar of light, its sheets and galaxies of airspray, the lower fringe vibrating with separate elastic bubbles – and there, shoulder to shoulder, nosing the refreshing shower, lay the trout, holding still, shrugging the current aside, adjusting with tail; one peeling lazily aside to take something bowled from above, then resuming position, the others fixed and staring, ever driving forward in the one place. They moved over to let me among them, myself kicking and pawing against the force ... and what was I waiting for in that timeless assembly, clutching so desperately at dismissive rock?

That world too, less visited now, is part of marginal gardening here, for the Burn is a kind of underwater path and I used to dam pools – pools were its compartments – to increase their depth and character; but we should move on again, out of the Gorge and across the next green tableland, down into the shady Dell for the final summer picture. Its theme, now rhododendrons are back to leaves, is principally of white and blue, set off by yellow, orange and an occasional dangerous carmine.

One large central bowl, possessing the rare advantage of a boggy floor, illustrates how planting modifies its rather unsubtle form. In late summer the sloping high banks carry luxuriant white veils from a line of tall arching shrubs which don't simply follow the rim but lift and fall along it in their own curves, at one point swinging down to the centre. These simple manoeuvres add mysterious depth to the place, the rim above and the floor below staying visible to hold all together. Piercing the white millinery, orange and yellow spires climb black-stemmed from great fingered leaves, a contrastingly stable and architectural base. The shrub's feathery panicles dazzle against blue sky and their hanging profusion, heavy with scent and clambering with bees, as a sight of August rivals that of heather across the Burn.[19]

Birds and animals disappear in summer behind scenery, but are heard in the wings – trundling of hedgehogs, mewing of buzzards, screams of kestrel and osprey, cackling of jays and woodpeckers; and the roding of a woodcock round its figure-of-eight evening beat: that nervous interrupted flutter and curious repetitive whimper and croak as it flits among birch glades is as familiar as the swift interwoven circuit of bats. Herons stalk the Burn, lazily lifting when disturbed and shepherding themselves away through protesting foliage.

Especially noticeable now are squirrels. They desert the pine wood, convenient earlier with its cones and canopy, for hazel coppice, where nuts rise small pale moons among yellowing leaves. This harvest attracts squirrels from far away, and commuters travel the Overground morning and evening across the fence; though residents usually get to work before them. Ancestors of these bushes, seed back through seed, probably also gladdened the Iron Age farmers whose hut circles litter the moors behind. Many hazels overhang the Burn itself, and bunches of white nuts, dropped by squirrels, float round its dark pools. In Celtic myth, the salmon of knowledge fed on nuts fallen from the nine hazels of poetic wisdom. Though these great fish ascend the river that the Burn joins, they rarely visit us. I go back at suitable times, hoping to recapture that unrepeatable first revelation.

> ...hasten, for the wind may soon
> unhook distraction, raining
> thick, the water move and break,
> the waterfall
> become uncertain, blown
> back to the rocks, unsteady.
>
> hasten, part the quiet unmown
> grasses carefully, and watch
> the pool. for not again
> will fathoms burn
> so lucidly for you, nor out of darkness
> hugely to you the rising silver turn. [1]

AUTUMN

In September, leaves begin to thin and make space. Even the days shorten and ripen.

Every clear morning grass and leaves bead with water, afternoons end sooner, and evenings carry a cold edge; shady places stay damp all day. Cloudless nights bring frost to the hill, and its bracken turns yellow further down the slopes each week. Birch leaves grow yellow, too, falling lightly on the paths, so that brown and amber trails wind through the green.

Summers can be unbelievably extended, with autumn two crippling nights that shred unhardened buds and stems; but this season is best when it approaches gently without sharp frost or wind, and takes its time to dismantle summer, tree by tree. Then, warm September sunlight throws pink shadows about wild blue scabious, and Small Tortoiseshell butterflies drink their last luxury; but for the chill in the grass, it could be a July afternoon. The sun slants lower each day between trees, illuminating areas shaded all summer, and the canopy lightens; a new brightness enters woodland. Colour comes back, as tired August greens sharpen to yellows and orange, washed lucent by rain.

Autumn can be our brightest period. Everywhere, from deep in the Gorge up to morning-frosted slopes of turf and heather, and everything, stem, leaf, berry and bud, wakens to a carnival of colour: yellow, orange, reds and purples glowing under long shadowed sunlight and violet clouds. Flowers become superfluous, not just to a restful garden, but to a brilliant one.

Most flowers are relics, flinching to brown as they open or scowling above dislocation. The herbaceous community is sad enough now, a last chapter in Proust. Fuchsia, an exception, enters more graciously into the geriatrics of autumn, scarlet and purple as ever, white dust of anthers still precise; as autumn withdraws about them, these bushes – urbane in formal surroundings, at ease in the wild – remain confident in their own extent of sun, comforting to have around the house; until the first considerable frost breaks and discards them.

This is also the time of gentians, smokily Plutonic as Lawrence could desire, but even these are survivors, torches going down, an interruption of the great slow swing towards winter. Autumn crocus rhymes better with the season, saying all it needs in naked unabashed, leafless, flower, then dying down. Not strayed from summer, it presages a change to austerity, and its simple bloom sends you ahead to snowdrops and the first clean blossoming of spring.

I must briefly sketch our autumn colours, though they cannot rival the more varied panoply of wealthier places. Our own incendiaries burn against silver-lichened boulders and the smouldering tones of surrounding hillsides; they ignite from acid-yellow moss through russet bracken to the fuming crimson of tall red oaks, and all display a simple zest, everyone sharing in the feast of leaf and berry.

So you are to imagine high skies of light blue, travelled by pale cirrus and washed by showers of cold rain. To the north clouds pile black and purple; from early October, hills are dusted white against them. Sounds echo crisp through the tang of autumn, that long after-taste of summer. And so do silences.

> *there are no silences*
> *in autumn silences,*
> *where you can hear a leaf fall*
> *on to other leaves*
> *and the wind blows silence in the bare boughs*
> *fiercely, and the river*
> *bundles its own silence over the rocks.*
>
> *what is that beating in my silence*
> *but the beat of the silence when it stops?* [1]

Birch is still our framework, its gold swimming above butter-yellow hazel, that yellow slapped on flat like butterpats, a still life beneath the flicker of birch. Below, too, is beech; all those hedges and miniature groves switch on their amber, orange and even purple and crimson at different rates, some yet green when others have run down to the last wet chestnut, a luminous harmony behind moss sprinkled with white, pink, olive and every whisper of red and brown. Beech, as dwarf woodland or intermittent bonfires beneath high conifer, is necessary as birch and hazel to autumn.

Outstanding also are blaeberry, running ruby and orange drifts between coal-black junipers and leathery rhododendrons; barberries, some an indescribable signal-red, orange-red berries enamelling their archings wands; and azaleas – with yellow, orange, scarlets, ruby-crimson and purples, darkening to deep blue, chasing across them, and central in each glaring rosette gleams next year's apple-green bud.

The lowest indispensable storey is bracken: an ochre, bleaching to cream, deepening to squirrel brown beneath the buttery hazels. When all leaves are down it dries to a foxy fur and loses its architecture; but that no longer matters, for the bones of the garden are visible again and bracken is free to add informal texture, across which pheasants saunter and crackle their own autumnal circumstance. Tiresome other times, these birds from their splendour this season find sanctuary here from ritual disturbance further down the glen.

> *a clatter of stained glass.*
> *that pheasant climbs*
> *red october air*
> *bracken-winged. who aims,*
> *crashing his gun, finds there*
> *blue smoke, gapped silence.*

see him go
carefully, not
look upward. he must know

he has broken a window. [1]

Many fine colourists of spring repeat their excellence in autumn. Larch opened shrill green and now closes with equally startling yellow, sharpening to bright orange, flattening to old gold, and falling away then softly; or vanishing altogether in one night of wind. An early snowfall drips glassily from its lime-green needles. Aspen, then liquid silver, now coins doubloons of real gold, a gilding distinct from orange and brown either side or any counterfeits of terracotta. Aspen gold here is up to Colorado standard, and from pale blue sky falls leisurely in handfuls, strewing the paths with an ample gesture of sovereigns. You kick richly through them.

I must dismiss our Sorbus species – whose finest season this is – in a single sentence reserved for one kind laden with ox-blood berries that pale to rose and then to bright almond-pink, while neat leaflets flush red, maroon, purple and finally bronze before falling and leaving the naked tree, bowed beneath its fruit, as astonishingly luminous in November (despite the fieldfares) as a flowering almond in early spring. [20]

In autumn, evergreen conifers step forward again to reassure you against winter. Those with a glaucous edge of silver about their needles best set off deciduous yellows and reds – Sitka spruce or Scots pine, for example, preferable to the greeny Norway spruce or lodgepole pine when fronting ripening hill-grass and blue distances. Fiercely pungent Sitka spruce, towering waxy blue behind red oak in tawny evening light, are memorable. Without conifers autumn would lose much of its excitement: just to walk under blue spruce and pine after leaving the orangey gold of larch and aspen is to taste the very air smoky, so overwhelming is the transformation about you.

63

In late autumn the air often smokes with rain, pelting the last leaves off trees and flooding the Burn, which rises fast. Heard from the house its rumble breaks to a bellow as you open the door. Beside it, your spine rattles to the thud and grind of travelling boulders and you smell that 'unforgettable, unforgotten' racing white water. No rock, cascade or pool is visible, just a huge rope belabouring the Gorge. At the garden bridge it is 35 feet across, pier to pier, its walloping fringe snuffling last summer's stems and blowing Guinness froth about your feet. When highest it makes least noise – a swift alarming *swoosh* – so much is then above boulders and bankside rocks; convex, bulging along the middle, a terrifying muscular punch. Dippers flit complainingly, but prudently, about the shaking banks.

Yet below all this, Himalayan primulas survive, reasserting themselves in spring through the boulders and shingle yearly redistributed around them. Tons of mica-schist are bullied downstream, but primulas preside over their summer in exactly the same place.[21]

After a spate, scenery has changed: fragile waterfalls abolished, cliffs dissolved to rapids. The lip of the big waterfall has retired upstream ten feet in thirty-five years, and a tower beside it likewise; summit hazels straddle with bare roots, and a sprucelet I pushed into its flat blaeberry top all those years ago is now a tall tree whose time has come, a foot from the plunging slab. A favourite deep-diving pool beneath is choked with fangs of rock, monstrous sharp-angled fragments scarred by impact, the wounded cliff peering from above; occasionally a birch stands on its head in the water, loose boulders collected on up-ended roots. Dynamic gardening, beside the Burn.

In heavy rain, it is good to lie on the dry soil of hut floors and watch the drops splashing and rolling off the various leaves and twigs, listening to the myriad songs, drinking with the roots, just watching, experiencing the weather; what is called 'bad' weather being as rich as fair periods and, in huts at any rate, more generously allowing any Antaeus his brute comfort of solid earth and a reconciliation to final union with it. Outside, given good rainproofs, maybe benches would serve, but never those of masonry....

> *...who would sit on*
> *marble, relax*
> *so near the bone?....* [4]

Too sudden and implausible here, where we unobtrusively position wooden ones, home-grown, and carry a square of featherweight insulating plastic to convert them and any stump, boulder or scoop of an earthy bank into two square feet of warm dry luxury; so that wet weather takes its place as a rightful partner throughout the year.

Leaves are beaten down with the rain, but there is pleasure in the very energy of leaflessness, not only from tall timber but also from what W. C. Williams described as

> *....the reddish*
> *purplish forked, upstanding twiggy*
> *stuff of bushes and small trees....*

Life is more evident now leaves are gone. Garden and gardener breathe more deeply.

> *it is good*
> *to return from exuberance,*
> *along with the weather*
> *to dead grass*
> *brown heather*
> *water clear enough*
> *where it is not frozen.*

August was too
bellyripe and breathless,
made scenes.
the children cried.
nothing demeans
like fecundity.
it is good to return to no leaves... [1]

So this season inspires a Protestant work ethic, a Permanent Reformation – 'Which always must be carried on/And still is doing but never done', as Butler puts it; for autumn anyway, and especially in marginal silviculture.

This playing with toy forests and shelterbelts entails thinning and planting, tasks which share out the weather, days too cold and dry for planting being good for thinning – of branches or trees. Thinning of dead branches, 'brashing' – cutting them off to above head height – wonderfully clears both wood and mind; new perspectives open once that clutter is removed.

Brashing is
lopping off dead branches, all
entanglement, outgrown

gesture; so your trees
rise calm and clean into their own
September. When

you leave them, go home
they resume
high business, needle on needle

repeating, gathering
the night wind; and
you do not mind

you do not look behind
at what's beginning again, what storm,
what growing collision of darkness.

You have no concern,
the job being done
and they putting up another season,

the tall leaders
quarrelling together
against their stars. [4]

You can identify a tree in the dark from its resistance to brashing, as well as from scent. Scented resin blackens sawblade and fingers, the very taste and smell of autumn.

Brashing conifers rolls up blinds, opens doors and windows, and the forest floor welcomes a succession of immigrants, increasing each year with the light. Before this, the pine wood resembled an empty factory, all views channelled down silent brown corridors of verticals, its only relief the texture and colour of passing trunks themselves. I planted the wood as tiny two-year-olds in open heather, which they choked as they grew up and linked arms above it; then paths had to be hacked through them, virgin bush.

I cut this trail
through young pine
they climb up past me
to the sun.

I make the same
journey too,
axeing darkness
here below

peering ahead
where no one has been,
either side
where no one will go. [1]

Now they are over 30 feet tall, I thin them to prevent crowding. This minute forest of an acre or so provides year-round
interest. Not managed primarily for shelter, it yields fuel, odd
structural timber and ecological diversity. I try, through a form
of 'selection thinning', to evolve and keep going a natural-look-
ing uneven-aged stand of mixed species: by removing selected
individuals, thinning the overcrowded to make room for seedlings beneath, and introducing new deciduous members. I don't
randomly mix species, but encourage groups for their own flora, and flavour; ensuring maximal amenity for animal life, including my own. So the pine wood carries now an increasing
lower storey of deciduous trees and bushes, all scathingly cate-
gorised by commercial foresters as 'weed species'. Stationed
nearby is an eager young commercial forest, pure Dynamo of
Henry Adams; his Miraculous Virgin herbicided to the other
side of the wire.

> *These are the trees*
> *that grow straight, seeds*
> *of knowledge, planted, fed*
> *tended line by line to be*
>
> *felled in a gale*
> *of sawdust and petrol. Not those*
> *over the fence, sown free*
> *broken by season, strays*
>
> *swarming with eyes and evasion*
> *pests and diseases, the wry*
> *birch and aspen, beautiful*
> *weed species.* [4]

Certainly, a well-grown strictly commercial forest is a fine –
though rare – accomplishment in its own right. Anyway, in the
interests of diversity and the White Goddess I stand and select
which trees to fell. Candidates are suppressed pine, stationary,

relinquishing their rights – for, being light-demanders, they will die – and those with curved unstable boles from too loose planting before snow-load. Dominant larches come down if not in larch areas, and any pine whose removal would strengthen a tall silvery-aspiring birch clasping it in close dancer's embrace (the lady reaching sunlight better than if standing back), unless separation would break down both partners, when I pass by, congratulatory. It is difficult to select 'largely pine' or 'largely birch' areas; in the centre of an otherwise 'largely birch' region will grow a superb pine, destined to kill off the birch. I keep pines with stout trunks and least imbalance, so that mutilation by snow will merely diversify the upper limbs to form – eventually – those typical open-ground 'Scottish' Scots pine of oak-like proportions seen in fragments of Caledonian Forest[22], behind dramas by Landseer, or loyally on tins of shortbread. Elsewhere in this garden I fell, say, good Douglas fir round a graceful birch apparently due years of life, which succumbs next winter, no longer being supported by coniferous neighbours: and nothing is left to fill the gap. Difficult.

Thinning dominates the vital fourth dimension of design and is usually – from lack of foresight or courage – left too late. Trees grow behind your back all of a sudden; yet their vertical scale must be controlled, their understorey not shaded out, and successors left room to rise. Otherwise you are condemned to draughty halls of poles and eventual clear-felling from desperation, or storm. You must ensure a range of heights, deciduous and evergreen, and in the right places. It is like maintaining a herbaceous border on a larger and less forgiving time scale; and needs more skills than managing a big block monoculture – or than I possess. I am always reluctant to disturb the status quo with *when?* and *which?* Not easy to decide.

When you do decide, lower branches are removed to allow access. Direction of fall must not damage neighbours or lodge the tree. You slice a 'bird's beak' notch in the trunk facing the chosen direction, so the final cut above it sets the tree in balance on a hinge bending that way.

Few things are more satisfying than seeing this cut open, switching off your saw, stepping back behind another tree and watching the trunk lurch, pause, crackle below, then topple with a surprisingly silent and rapid *swish* through foliage to THUMP! shockingly on the ground.

> *so*
> *it is down.*
> *sawn up and gone.*
> *a huge absence*
> *as after thunder.*
> *neighbouring branches*
> *stretch and explore,*
> *blackbirds, thrushes*
> *kick up the finger bones,*
> *I for my share*
> *watch that great head swinging*
> *dizzy with memory.*
>
> *and know my bare eyes*
> *the poor october things they are.* [1]

Then you look round to see if the new gap meets approval. Like accidental wind-throw, it often seems an improvement, sometimes a great one, any rawness balanced by floods of light and the comfort that young growth smooths things over. It is creation at a stroke, this destruction: you have rejuvenated the garden, revealed a new distance to be incorporated, changed gear into the next equilibrium.

You visit the site daily, as a minor triumph. A mistake is also eyed repeatedly; usually due to belated felling, it will take years to repair. I resist taking out more trees right away, as if to drown the sudden hole in a greater emptiness; you need a cool head, with such a balancing of time above it. Any disaster due to storm will have been predicted and new vistas prepared beforehand; yet those losses are usually of great old trees that contributed the weight of centuries.

I bark conifers after felling, to prevent insect pests. As the moist strips peel off, ivory bones appear, darkening and drying within the day, threads of stray cambium curling and weathering around them like raffia.

Thinning well done, timber stacked gleaming in neat array and its brush great green heaps for future mulch – this is a joy of autumn.

Planting is another. On our diminutive scale, short rotations of planting and felling are best. The felled trees are small enough at 50 to 60 feet to be manoeuvrable, yet tall enough to provide timber for huts and fences, or good firewood; sawdust, brush and bark add to the soil. Their small replacements ensure continual supply of delightful young trees for low shelter and colour. You help to bowl the hoop, the cycle, the Wheel.

> *he often wrote about*
> *felling trees*
> *and planting them.*
>
> *as when he cut down*
> *a fifty foot larch*
> *he put there at nine inches*
>
> *and planted a pine*
> *at four and a half. that*
> *is not to create.*
>
> *it is what he was writing about.*
> *a weeping of forests*
> *from one genesis.* [2]

With short rotations I know the history of each post and beam of the various huts about the place; when two supports of a woodshed were a great swaying larch; and before, when they were a promise in its pencil of a stem overtopped and tweaked by a child in blue woollies – whose car is parked beside the woodshed and whose own next generation inspects a further line of young larch. Time is of little consequence; there is every reason for planting trees even when it is closing in. I continue, beyond the years of discretion, to afforest strips outside the garden proper; although I shall scarcely have the chance to see them check even a breeze.

> *... Plant on,*
> *chance has season.*
> *This is autumn*
> *without question.*
>
> *Tall the oak,*
> *rough its bark.*
> *Its roots*
> *consume silence.* [4]

Late autumn settles into winter. Leaves choke pools and ditches, pile against boulders in the Burn. I collect them in a bucket for mulch. One morning the leaves are bladed with glass and the bucket rattles. Overhead, clouds have parted and ice-blue tongues of sky lick in the winter. Now deciduous canopy has gone, clear nights bring back regular frosts. Cold air brushes past, stirring bamboos in the Dell; bamboos have not rustled on a calm evening since early June.

The brief walk-round is complete. November is here and 'Winter' again. Ash leaves are down, hazel leaves in heaps, poplar leaves sunk in the pool; its surface is starred with pondskaters feeding on drowned bees. Down there, all is dank and quiet with Stevens'

> *...silence*
> *Of a sort, silence of a rat come out to see.*

Earth rings as if empty. We know it is not. There are swelling and thrusting of roots, seeds stirring, bright eyes about hoards – everyone is busy deep down. The gardener stamps cold feet on thin crust, goes back to his house. From its doorway on crystal evenings he sees the Aurora Borealis shuttling far-off orange, green and red, stark electronics of the season. Against that cosmic bravado the silhouetted branchwork draws closer, next year's catkins plump and confident.

Autumn is a powerful time, calling out and testing all in garden and gardener. A kind of transfiguration before the end.

Good to go off in colours.
Scarlet before the sleet;
fuming crimson, shrieking orange,
a relaxed butterpat

yellow. Name them. Anything
is better than flat
worn-out green. Even that
is strangely remote

in frost lying on the white
grass, whiter
edged, each vein
picked out for the last time, crystalline. 4

CROP

Back in the house, the lamp can be lit. I must try to relate this kind of gardening to gardening in general, and to the rest of the ecosystem, including ourselves.

Firstly, then, what is a 'garden', and the activity called gardening?

Gardening is a property of living systems: those of the garden and of the gardener. It is as elusive to define as life itself. Life, one can suppose, did not clearly differentiate from the non-living matrix until a simple bounding membrane enclosed it and it became a cell. The membrane was semi-permeable and allowed selection of what went in and what went out. This island in the flux could then initiate its own directed flux, interdependent with the external largely random one; it became a living system extracting energy from its environment to maintain its own equilibrium, and to grow. Beginning – or joining – the creative exploration passed on to us.

Similarly, a garden is not differentiated from the wild (or from someone else's garden) until it has a fence round it, or some other manifestation of the gardener's intent – grass clipped here, a plant set there, or a weed defined and pulled out. It is then launched on its course and will continue as long as the gardener, that most practical of Berkeleians, wills it.

For, deprived of his wish, the garden must cease to exist as surely as a cell that loses its energy and membrane. A garden cannot function without committed human participation. As Wallace Stevens pointed out,

> *... The rose, the delphinium, the red, the blue,*
> *Are questions of the looks they get...*

Now, why a garden should function at all is possibly best understood by considering *how* it functions. A garden may be thought of as governed by four factors, summarised in the diagram, where G represents the garden and the arrows are the four factors.

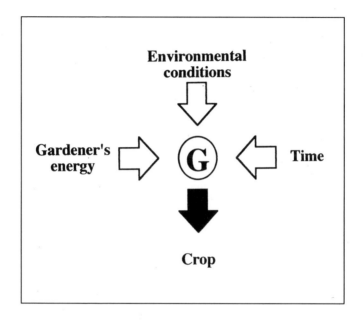

Three factors concern input, and one, output. The three of input are: *environmental conditions* - as of sun, soil, stresses and suchlike; *gardener's energy* – the gardener's own input of ideas, finance and labour; and *time* – the period of growth of the garden in the gardener's mind, and on the site. The factor of output is the *crop* itself. This crop – the reason for the garden – can be for physical need of the gardener, as food, fuel or commercial produce; or for psychical need, as pleasure in sight, scent and mental or physical activity; or for any combination of these.

The importance of individual arrows may be independently

varied and if the model were pursued and programmed sophisticatedly it could define any given garden, or other exploration, generating much innocent employment.

Now, I termed this particular garden a Marginal Garden. What *is* a marginal garden? How will the diagram 'define' it? A marginal garden is, I suggest, minimally differentiated from its environment, minimally costed energy-wise, and nowadays usually cropped for pleasure. The nature of the environment, and time, are the only variables. If the environment were urban, a marginal garden would be minimally differentiated from the surrounding stonework and paving; and, incurring minimal energy, could be very formal indeed. A marginal garden can be made anywhere and to any degree of formality, consistent with minimal input of energy. My own garden is on wild hillside, and if it were transposed in its present form into a cultivated, suburban or urban landscape it would no longer be marginal, for more effort would be needed to make, maintain and accept it there. Obviously, every wild garden is not necessarily a marginal one, for there are degrees of rural 'wildness' and to be marginal a wild garden must mate with its local wildness, whether on a Sutherland moor or a Cambridgeshire meadow. Such gardens, easily made and maintained, are set to increase throughout Europe as small farms continue to be broken up and more people move out from towns to work at home in relaxed surroundings.

The other variable in the case, Time, may extend over the lives of great trees or annuals within a season; neither it nor its co-ordinate Space dictates whether or not a garden will be marginal.

Enough, I think, on defining marginality; although the obliging diagram, having room for any area bounded by Intent, will even accommodate an apparently unmanaged Nature Reserve – marginal in the extreme – where human energy input is largely intellectual, as is the crop. For no reserve can, from its very name, have been without intent originally just as no garden or any area deliberately utilising only indigenous vegetation of local provenance, can truly be termed 'natural'. 'Natural' this year is not 'natural' two hundred years ago before our rabbits moved up, or seven hundred years ago when wild pigs prepared nursery beds, or even last year, when there were elms; and cosmopolitan spores and seeds have been raining in on wind, feathers, feet and Import Crates ever since the glaciers went back.

Fortunately, a *garden* need not worry about its managerial or alien status. Our crop need only satisfy ourselves: as the indispensable Miss Jekyll, with often averted eye, studiously maintained – 'one must not quarrel with it, because a garden is for its owner's pleasure....'

To sum up, the diagram demonstrates how gardening must intimately root together the physical, intellectual and imaginative: inputs of both spade and drawing board, outputs of both fragrant delight and earnest documentation – the last maybe an endearing attempt to press the flux into some dry herbarium keepsake, nostalgically tagged. *Campanula latifolia* 'Alba', for example, a shade-bearing drought-resisting perennial,

is a tall
steeple of white bells climbing,
a carillon

with purple echoes at the throat,
rooted
in a rosette of devoted leaves

chiming
peal after peal crystal
through June evenings until

petals are shed
and globes of green seed
hang silent below.

Then the name will make do.
It is tied to the stem every season,
and tries to ring true. [4]

The previous pages have, I hope, suggested how a marginal wild garden exemplifies, more strikingly than a conventional garden could, this union of aesthetic appreciation and biological knowledge – or, as the explorer would put it, of artistic endeavour and scientific enquiry. For the biomass (a pleasingly inclusive term) that you meet there is not readily persuadable. Its ingredients have fought among themselves, making and breaking alliances, for maybe thousands of years on that site to reach their present tranquillity; and interference – however marginal – provokes immediate reaction: it obstructs maybe a vital botanical or zoological manoeuvre and, by helping some plants and hindering others, can unchain green murder.

Because you interfere only when you have to, and with least disturbance, you learn to study the life of plant and animal, ally and competitor; you realise your human responsibility and power of compassion, on this vigorous battlefield; how to carry safely and use to the minimum, your saw, snare and gun or your new chemical weapons, which are so crude compared with the delicately murderous molecular armoury concealed about you in fiercely rivalsome root, leaf and blossom. You begin to understand why good design grows from this knowledge; why wood anemone drifts only over a certain soil under a certain density of birches, and never under spruce; why oak fern sheets one side of a ridge, woodrush the other; and why any attempt to transgress such bounds looks wrong, and fails, for the same reason. Plants in this kind of garden, like the Blackface ewes beyond the fence, know their own hill best and the gardener is very much a shepherd, to help them in crises, encourage them here or there, but never to drive them overmuch.

As shepherd, he is himself part of the biomass, wholly involved in the landscape he guides; plant, animal and man interact with site and seasons.

The gardener, like the rat, pursues personal 'pleasure'. Yet he seeks a composite one – sensory, intellectual, imaginative, moral – a human pleasure. He takes the wilderness, a complexity arising from what could be called chance, and directs it like a human life, exploring, observing and choosing for that composite pleasure. In my own case I believe this unity of approach allows glimpses of a kind of beatitude: of that inner calm paced about by the great pibrochs; cradled beneath the monstrous thrusts and counterthrusts of Gothic cathedrals; or bared by a simple act of charity. I am aware in a wild marginal garden of the immanence of vast rooted forces, flowering about me; and it seems good to be able to share in this a little, even with no more than a spade.

Marginal gardening here, then, you cannot suffer long from the mirage of self-sufficiency. Nor from absurd compartmentalisation of enquiry into that of 'scientist' or 'artist' or whatever. And certainly not from anarchic sentimentality.

> *who is that*
> *among our butterflies*
> *trading the wrong laughter?*
> *he does not even distract them.*
> *they punctuate flowers*
> *yellow and blue*
> *without him, prefer*
>
> *a defined view,*
> *cooler articulation. visit*
>
> *leopardsbane*
> *milk vetch; meadow rue.* [1]

Yourself, long integrated with your own cultural ecosystem, might, among tall trees in spring, hear with Lawrence 'the slow powerful sap drumming in their trunks'; with Gertrude Jekyll[23] appreciate how through these 'birch stems... the value of the careful colour scheme of the rhododendrons is fully felt...'; and pass on to judge from experience which of the two opposing forces – the hatch of the *Aphidecta* ladybird in the warm sun, or the strength of the desiccating northwest wind – will decide the fate of this year's aphid onslaught on young and over-sanguine Douglas firs. You inevitably learn more about yourself from being part of this complex interdependence, which it has always been foolish, and now appears dangerous, to ignore.

Indeed, one fascination of making a garden is the unintentional finding out of more about yourself; to discover yourself making it to your own idea of order, as those made elsewhere in place and time reflected other ideas of order: Nonesuch, Stowe, Versailles, Granada or – more strictly still – the various dogmatic gardens of Japan, of temple, imperial villa or shogun's palace.

Let me – for I must return to the self-referential, not from solipsism, but because this book concerns personal exploration – conclude by relating this garden to its own gardener: what has it to do with *me*? Why did *I* make it, and here of all places?

Perhaps the simpler, the more marginal, the garden, the more unobstructedly you realise yourself in its design. I suppose I realise myself in the very choice of site – high-latitude, high-altitude, exposed – and its bare basal accompaniment of boulders and rock-exploring trees, tight precise minimal flowers; life and its reflections battered and burnished to concentrate the intrinsic inner – sweetness, peace? – what shall we say? Crystal? If so, not a withdrawal of life, an inorganic abstraction, but a packed essence of the force behind the flux, a seed, preserver of the unity of being.

> *dry leaves*
> *under the hazels.*
> *bare stems, stirring.*
> *a bare wind*
>
> *and a bare sun*
> *on a bare day*
> *dropped into winter.*
> *no sound.*

no birds about.
and a hazel tree
in the hazel nut
on my bare hand. [1]

Perhaps that is why I have explored and written – often in verse of maybe their own character – about such things: mountains, forests, seas and their human horizons, the twisted beauty of Scotland, its urban crags and boulderfields ... and the seed within them.

the high flats at Craigston stand
rawboned in a raw land,
washed by thunderstorm and sun
and cloud shadows rolling on

from the bare hills behind, each one
out-staring the wind;
that every night
cling together and tremble with light. [2]

I could in fact argue that making this garden is writing a poem, and walking the paths, reading it. And like a poem, only partly composed by oneself; the structure is there, waiting to offer its message, to be framed as 'epiphanies', compartments of happening, to communicate with the planter – who will fit his plants to it like words chosen (Emily Dickinson's 'candidates') for the correct place, and delete the weeds; and through his planting maybe to communicate with others, as I suggested earlier when 'defining' verse. The result, dimly imagined, sometimes astonishes when the sun lights it. Or there could be several poems, one for each axis, the cross-paths reflections between them... Whatever the reason, I walk this square of land, the last station of the quest, and call it a 'garden', a place of seeds.

And when time sends a garden, any garden, back to the matrix, it is not nullified; it has, as I said, *been*; is imprinted, however privately, on the matrix. But I am not going, here, beyond that particular margin.

This garden will, I think, 'ruin well'. Unlike the monumental tyrannies of the hapless Speer, it was not consciously so designed; but the site, that has seen to much, will see to that. Left ten years, a century – 'undeveloped' of course if that be possible – a succeeding owner could guide it back to much the same garden as it is now, from what would still be the same soil, exposure and topography and pretty much the same wild vegetation. In which case a fine opportunity exists, for translation: of this garden as poem, made over into someone else's personal language. A pity I shall miss it.

I close with another extract from Stevens, to whom life gave a chance for 'fictive creation' within very restrictive margins, and for whom also plant and landscape symbolised a peculiarly personal relationship with this planet. It is from *The Poem That Took the Place of a Mountain*, but would equally illustrate a garden taking the place of a poem. Every garden, as every exploration, is the signature of its maker on the earth; however clumsy or marginal, it therefore deserves reverence. Stevens' lines describe, I believe, what the garden discussed in these pages came to mean for its maker; and how he began to understand, after many years, what he was, as tenant, trying to do.

... How he had recomposed the pines,
Shifted the rocks and picked his way among clouds,

For the outlook that would be right
Where he would be complete in an unexplained completion:

The exact rock where his inexactnesses
Would discover, at last, the view towards which they had edged.

NOTES

These Notes concern: *Sources of verse* quoted without acknowledgement in text; *localisation* of less familiar topographical examples; *identification of plants* that were particularly noted. More detailed horticultural accounts of this garden, with photographs, will be found in *The Garden* (Journal of the Royal Horticultural Society): 113, 81–87 (Feb 1988), 512–518 (Nov 1988); 116, 269–273 (May 1991), 326–330 (Jun 1991); 117, 14–15 (Jan 1992), 184–185 (Apr 1992), 316–317 (Jul 1992), 474–475 (Oct 1992); 118, 72–74 (Feb 1993), 198–200 (May 1993); 368–370 (Aug 1993), 520–521 (Nov 1993); 119, 126–127 (Mar 1994), 268–270 (Jun 1994), 414–415 (Sep 1994), 578–579 (Dec 1994).

1. From *Camp One*, G. F. Dutton (M. Macdonald, Edinburgh, 1978); now o.p., but signed copies still available (£4.50 post paid) via Menard Press.
2. From *Squaring the Waves*, G. F. Dutton (Bloodaxe Books, Newcastle, 1986).
3. Cuillin Ridge, Loch Scavaig: adjacent natural features on the Isle of Skye, Scotland.
4. From *The Concrete Garden*, G. F. Dutton (Bloodaxe Books, Newcastle, 1991).
5. Hidcote, Gloucestershire and Sissinghurst, Kent, England: gardens made in the first half of the 20th century, respectively by Lawrence Johnston, and by V. Sackville-West and H. Nicolson.
6. From a translation by K. H. Jackson, *A Celtic Miscellany*, (Routledge and Kegan Paul, London, 1951).
7. Mons Graupius, A.D. 83, battle won by Romans in unsuccessful attempt to impose a *Pax Romana* north of the (later) Antonine Wall; Forteviot, A.D. 843, a possible site of the final Pictish defeat by the Scots; Culloden, A.D. 1746 – no comment required.
8. The poet William Shenstone punctuated the paths of his extensive wild 'lanskip' garden at The Leasowes, near Birmingham, England, with urns, obelisks and exhortatory verses.
9. From published uncollected verse, G. F. Dutton.
10. Translated by Robin Fulton, in *Olav Hauge, Selected Poems*, (White Pine Press, Fredonia, N.Y., USA, 1990).
11. *Rhododendron rex.*
12. *Rhododendron luteum.*
13. *Rhododendron fortunei* x *griffithianum.*

14. *Heracleum mantegazzianum* (Taxon A of McClintock).
15. *Rosa sericea.*
16. *Rosa moyesii.*
17. *Calluna vulgaris.*
18. See *Swimming Free*, G. F. Dutton (Heinemann, London, 1972, o.p.)
19. *Holodiscus discolor.* Beneath are *Ligularia* 'Gregynog Gold' and 'The Rocket'.
20. *Sorbus vilmorinii.*
21. *Primula florindae.*
22. Rapidly disappearing natural stands of *Pinus sylvestris* var. *scotica.*
23. The contribution of Gertrude Jekyll, theoretical and practical, not only to gardening and architecture but to the arts in general, as well as to craftsmanship and ecology, is now appreciated and her writings are being widely reprinted. Her first book *Wood and Garden* (Longmans, London, 1899) is probably the best introduction to one who frequently appears in the text and whose juxtaposition with DHL is by no means a confrontation of opposites.

EPILOGUE

Several plants in the marginal garden just described were first discovered, or collected, by George Forrest. It would seem a suitable Epilogue to a book of exploration, therefore, to reproduce below verses which commemorate Forrest, and which at the same time bring together from a wide range of sources the various interweaving strands – physical, scientific, aesthetic, spiritual – that supported the more personally examplified Quest of the preceding pages. They make up the same rope, and demonstrate its toughness.

Forrest was one of the greatest plant collectors. On his first trip, to the Tibetan border of Yunnan in 1904, at that time torn by Lamaist uprisings, he frequently faced unpleasant death. The French Jesuits with whom he was staying were slaughtered and he himself escaped only after a desperate journey alone, hunted by men and dogs. Undeterred, he returned and between then and 1932 sent back, from further explorations, dried samples and living seeds of a great number of species, very many of them new. Born at Falkirk, Scotland, in 1873, short, stocky, sparing of speech, with a keen sense of humour and little time for fools, he won immense respect by his courage, application and common sense. He, of course, never needed to search the upper snows; he measured his own Everests.

It is not inappropriate to note that several of the brave Jesuit missionaries themselves not only sowed their seeds of Faith into these storms, but gathered and despatched to Europe, also from the Love of God, botanical collections of outstanding scientific value and beauty.

here are the gorges,
mekong, yangtze, salween,
yellow between
long green
shudders of the himalaya.

up from the boil,
the steam,
to the stone bowl of the snow line climb
the rhododendron jungles, toil-
ing back into silence. here the

great waxed separate
primitive scented
blossoms, white, white
studded with crimson, gold, blood-
red, rising slowly, shed
monsoons from elephant leaves,
fictolacteum
irroratum, vernicosum, each receives
tapping of sunlight on
long-deliberated petals. here

his kindly host
old Père Dubernard dispensed
communion, was taken.
out from the smooth trunks praying
both arms broken,
robbed of nose and eyes,
picked naked to pieces
three nights and days,
staked in the ashes
of his mission. here

the so precious
seeds
were gathered up, despatched
according to the needs
of the distant professors,
the business men
with large crying gardens. here
he died
'on his last trip', satisfied,
suddenly, beside
his dog, his gun and a pheasant.
is buried
at tengyueh. here

because
india butts asia,
summits rise
brokenly
metre by metre
into untenable skies,
clutching their ice together,
and the great trees,
the extended stigmata,
ride obediently
up the steep valley. here

the snow plume flies
continually
over the last white stations,
over the icefall, twisted alloy,
limestone fossils, cylinders, ropes,
fluttering shreds
of the expedition tents. [1]